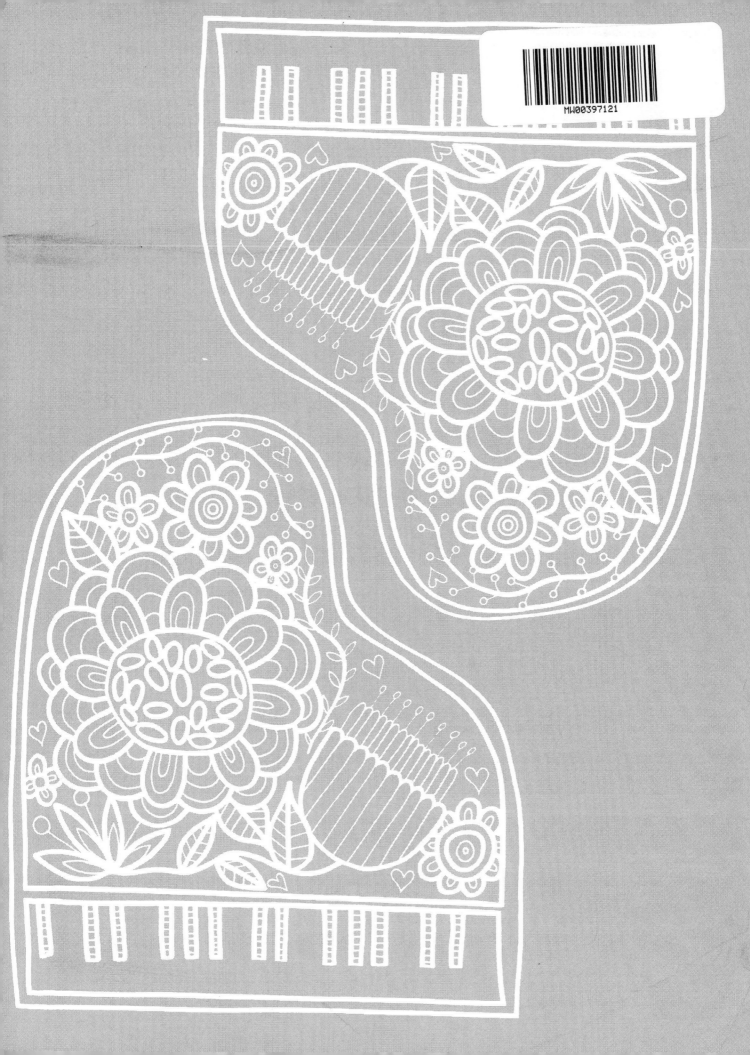

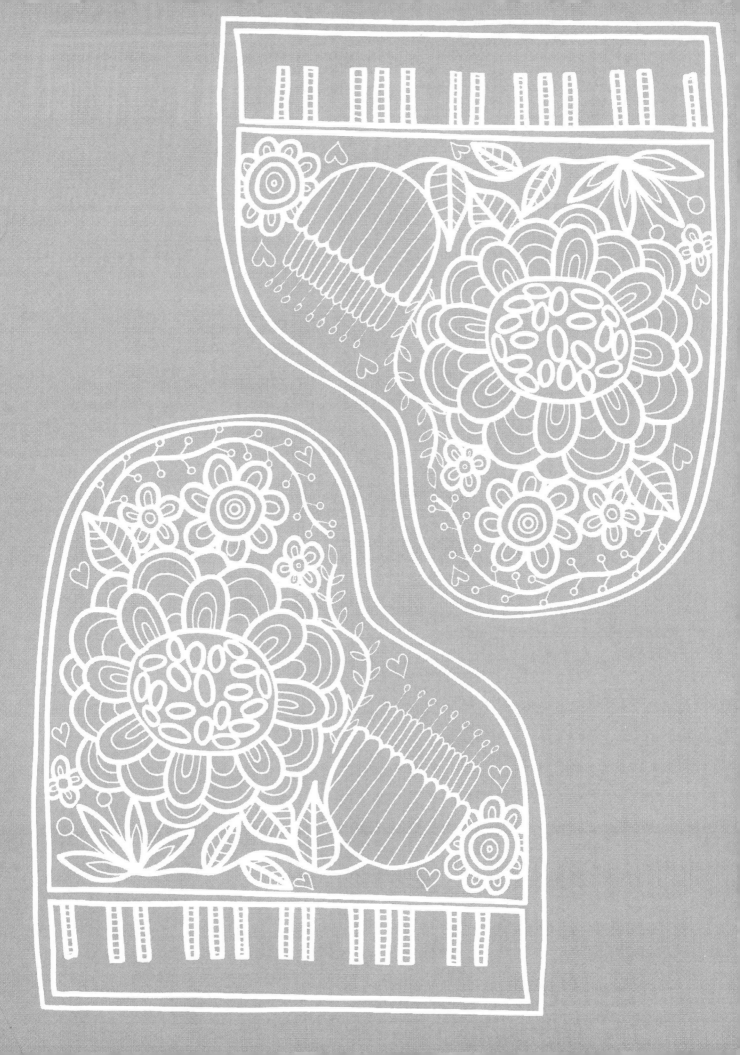

SHADES of SOUND
Women Composers

A LISTENING & COLORING BOOK FOR PIANISTS

by

Jennifer Boster, NCTM

SHADES OF SOUND
Women Composers

A Listening & Coloring Book for Pianists

By Jennifer Boster, NCTM

Copyright ©2018 Jennifer Boster
The Playful Piano | theplayfulpiano.com

ISBN: 9781726771290

The Playful Piano
PO Box 12931
Ogden, UT 84412-2931
USA

To my three favorite girls –
Ella, Norah & Annie

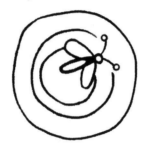

Table of Contents

Introduction

My goal in creating the Shades of Sound listening curriculum is to help piano students gain an interest in and a love and appreciation for great classical music.

Aspiring pianists need to know the literature, hear the greats perform, and be inspired and excited by the great music that is available! Just as writers need to read, read, read, pianists need to listen! Through this fun curriculum, students will learn about the great composers and their works. Listening repertoire selected includes selections from the solo piano literature, as well as piano and orchestra literature, and orchestral works.

My hope is that students can add just 5-10 minutes of listening per day to their normal practicing. Listening to great music will change their understanding of music and will vastly increase their music history knowledge. It will excite and inspire them, encourage further study and listening, give them new pieces to add to their own repertoire wish list, infuse more great music into their lives, homes and families, and will boost their musicianship and expression to the next level.

Women Composers

This volume of the series focuses on nineteen great women composers, spanning from the Medieval era to the present day. These women are talented and inspiring and deserve to be known and for their music to be heard and performed. I hope you have as much fun discovering these wonderful works as I did!

How to Use This Book

Read

Read each composer's biography to learn about their life and works. The Listening Selections page introduces the pieces you will hear and asks a couple of questions that you can answer as you listen.

Listen

Search for and pull up **"The Playful Piano – Women Composers"** playlist on YouTube (or scan this handy QR code!). All selections included in this book are in that list in the same order they appear here. I have chosen videos for each selection that are of good quality and will be inspirational and educational.

As you listen, rate each piece by coloring in the stars on the Listening Selections page. Five stars means "I loved this piece so much!" and one star means "I didn't really care for this piece." My hope is that students will find things to learn and appreciate about each selection, whether it becomes a favorite piece or not.

Color

As you listen to each piece, have fun coloring the accompanying coloring page! Jot down any notes or thoughts and answer the questions on the Listening Selections page.

Create a Repertoire Wish List

On page 10 I have included a blank "Repertoire Wish List" for students to use as they complete the listening assignments. This is a place for students to record pieces that they absolutely love and would love to learn someday! I hope that students will get excited about the rich variety of piano repertoire available and be inspired to learn some of the pieces they hear.

Happy Listening!

—Jennifer Boster

ThePlayfulPiano.com

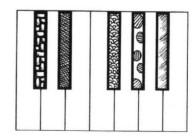

Repertoire Wish List

Pieces I have heard and would LOVE to learn!

Piece Title	Composer

Hildegard von Bingen

1098-1179
Germany

Hildegard von Bingen was a nun who lived in Germany during the Middle Ages. She was an abbess, which means she was in charge of the **convent** of nuns where she lived. She is one of the first identifiable composers in the entire history of Western music.

Hildegard was born the tenth child of a noble family. It was customary for families to promise their tenth child to the church as a **tithe**, so when she was around eight years old she was sent to live in an isolated hilltop monastery. Growing up in such an isolated convent in a single cell near the church, Hildegard grew up hearing the **chants** of the Roman mass. Her only musical training was in singing, but she must have learned a lot from listening. Hildegard became head of the convent in 1136 and began composing music for her nuns to sing. Aside from being a composer, Hildegard is also known as a visionary, a prophet, and a writer. She advised popes, emperors and kings through letters. She wrote books about medicine, biology, botany, theology and the arts.

Her music is in the style of **plainsong**, which is unaccompanied church music sung in unison. Plainsong uses medieval modes and a free rhythm. Hildegard's music is very **melismatic** and has a large range. She wrote original poetry as the text to much of her music. She believed that all of the music she composed was a result of God's inspiration.

Her musical works include a **liturgical** cycle of seventy-seven lyric **monophonic** poems, and a morality play made up of eighty-two melodies.

Kyrie (3 minutes)

Hildegard put the traditional Kyrie text from the mass to music, using a large range of more than an octave. This piece is unique because it has the sound of a major **mode**, a melodic practice that was not fully developed for three more centuries. Listen for her use of melisma, which is the movement through several notes on a single syllable of text.

Rate this piece: ★☆☆☆☆

What I like about this piece:	How I would describe this piece:

Ave generosa (6 ½ minutes)

This beautiful song is a hymn to the virgin Mary.

Rate this piece: ★☆☆☆☆

What I like about this piece:	How I would describe this piece:

13

Elisabeth Jacquet de la Guerre

1665-1729
France

Elisabeth Jacquet de la Guerre was a composer, teacher and **harpsichordist** who was born in Paris in 1665. She was one of the earliest professional female musicians. Maurice Hinson calls her "perhaps the most successful female French composer of all time."

She came from a family of musicians and instrument makers. Elisabeth was a child **prodigy**. Her first music teacher was probably her father, who was a harpsichordist, organist at a church and a harpsichord maker. It was not common at that time for fathers to support their daughters in a musical career; her father's influence likely helped her to eventually perform for **King Louis XIV** and get her professional career started. She had her first performance for the royal court around the age of twelve, singing and accompanying herself on the harpsichord. She became a member of the court and lived amongst the king's children and received an education.

Being in this position helped Elisabeth to be able to get much of her music published, as Louis XIV had complete control over music printed in France. Most of her pieces were dedicated to him, assuring that they would, in fact, be published. Her professional success was highly unusual for a woman of her day. Some think that she was somewhat of a rebel in her profession, and that coupled with the support from the king allowed her much success and artistic freedom.

As a performer, Elisabeth was skilled at **improvisation**. She was remarkably skilled and was well-known in France during her lifetime.

Jacquet de la Guerre is known for composing the first French opera written by a woman. Her works include two books of harpsichord suites (the first being published when she was just twenty-one years old), works for violin and **viola da gamba, cantatas,** and an opera.

Elisabeth married an organist, and contrary to the usual social practice of the time, continued to pursue her music career after her marriage. They had one son. Both her husband and son died in 1704, after which Elisabeth supported herself with her music.

Pieces de Clavecin, 1707 – Suite in D Minor

La Flamande (9 ½ minutes)

This is the first movement in a suite of harpsichord dance pieces. These pieces are intricate and dignified. Listen for the complex **ornaments** (trills, tremolos, grace notes, etc.) that are present in this style of music.

Rate this piece: ★ ☆ ☆ ☆ ☆

What I like about this piece:	How I would describe this piece:

Sonata in D minor

for violin, viola da gamba and **basso continuo** (16 minutes)

In Jacquet de la Guerre's time, the **sonata** was a new type of music and, particularly in France, was seen as somewhat suspicious. Because sonatas originated in Italy and because the violin (which often played a prominent role in sonatas of the day) was seen as a lesser or lowly instrument, sonatas were looked down upon in French society. However, Jacquet de la Guerre championed this new innovative music, being one of the first to write sonatas in France. In fact, when her sonatas were printed she dedicated them to King Louis XIV, who surprisingly liked her music even though he usually disliked new music.

Listen for the contrast between movements, from slow and expressive to quick and lively.

Rate this piece: ☆☆☆☆☆

What I like about this piece:

How I would describe this piece:

The Palace of Versailles, where Elisabeth performed for the king

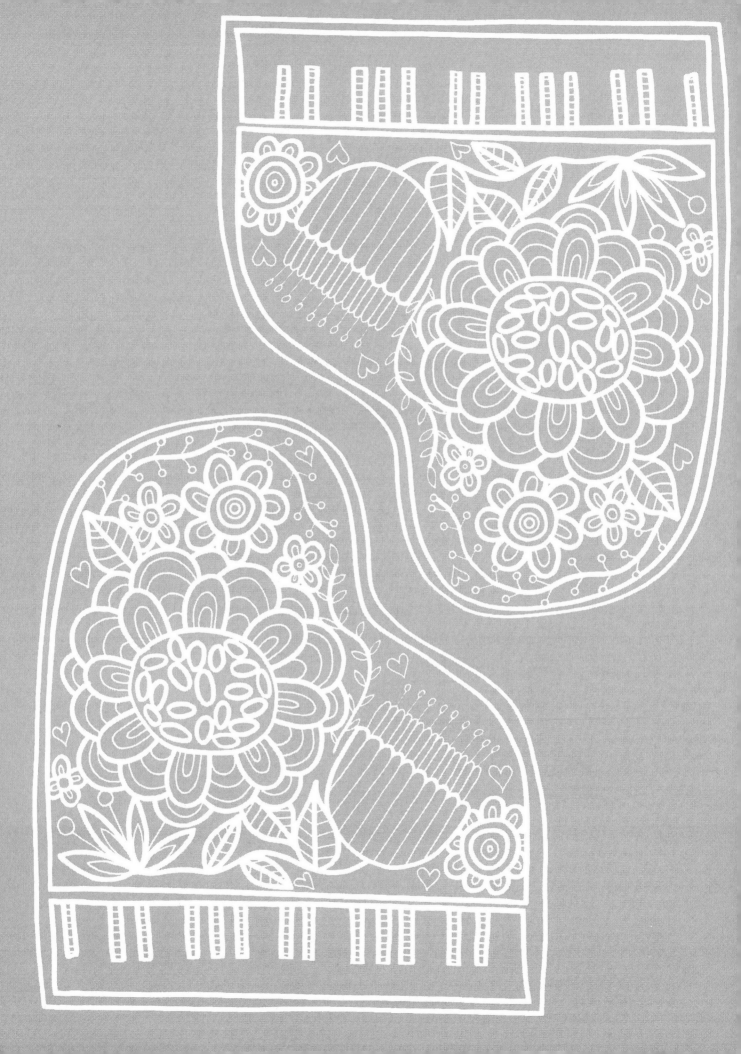

Maria Hester Park

1760-1813
England

Maria Hester Park was a British pianist, singer, composer and piano teacher. She was one of the most prolific of eighteenth-century female composers. She was friends with Haydn, with whom she corresponded through letters. They would often send each other pieces they had written. Her music was very popular in English drawing rooms; her compositions were the sort of music performed in Jane Austen novels. She taught piano lessons to members of the nobility. As a composer she was professional and very competent. Her compositions spanned a quarter of a century and include keyboard sonatas and a concerto for keyboard and strings.

When Maria married she ended her performing career. She and her husband had six children and had a very happy marriage.

Piano Sonata in C Major, Op. 7

I.   Allegro spirito (8 ½ minutes)
II.   Larghetto (3 minutes)
III.   Rondo: Allegramente (4 minutes)

This sonata begins with a quick and spirited first movement. The middle movement is slower and very beautiful. The final movement is a rondo. The style of this sonata is very Classical, in fact it sounds very similar to Mozart's piano sonatas.

Rate this piece: ☆☆☆☆☆

What I like about this piece:	How I would describe this piece (Allegro spirito):

How I would describe this piece (Larghetto):	How I would describe this piece (Rondo: Allegramente):

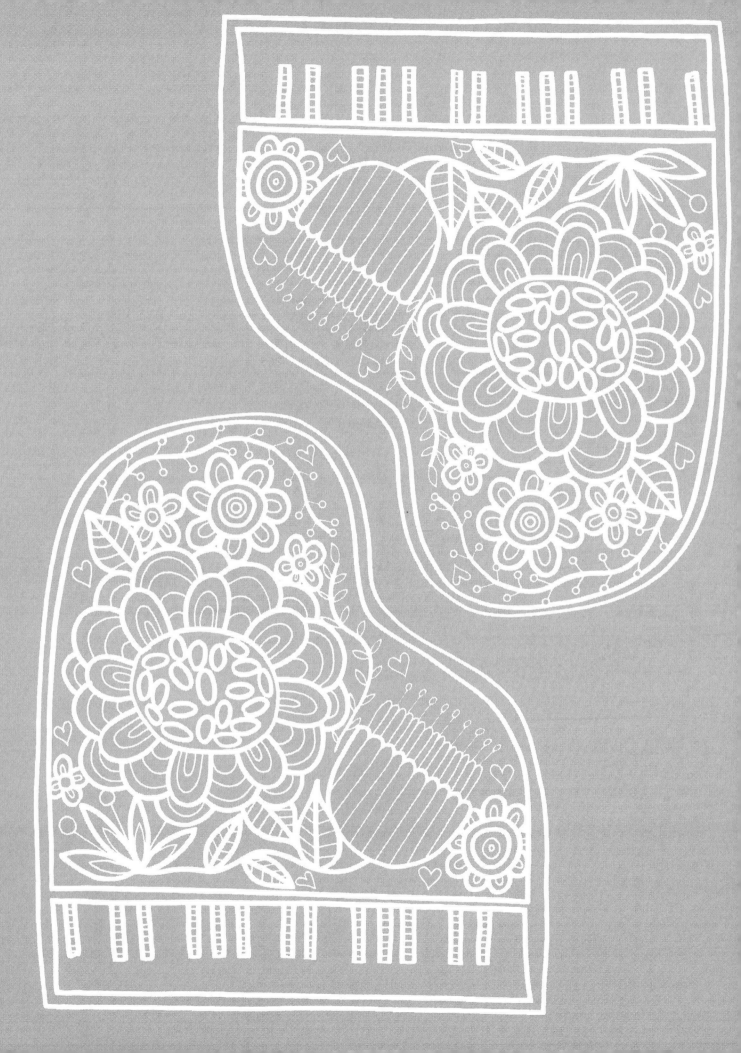

Marie Bigot

1786-1820
France

Marie Bigot was a French pianist, piano teacher and composer who was known for her sonatas and etudes. She grew up in a musical family – her parents played the cello and the piano. Her mother was her first piano teacher, beginning when Marie was around the age of five. She was an extraordinary musician who was acquainted with many famous composers. She taught piano to both Felix and Fanny Mendelssohn as well as Franz Schubert. She was friends with and frequently performed works by both Haydn and Beethoven. After hearing her play one of his pieces, Haydn said, "My dear child, that is not my composition; you have not simply played it, you have written it." In 1805 she sightread in concert Beethoven's *Appassionata* sonata from his **manuscript**, which Beethoven later gave to her.

Marie's husband was taken prisoner for five years during the Napoleonic Wars, during which time she was able to support herself and her two children with her teaching. Marie performed in both public and private venues and even ran her own **salon**. Bigot's playing was described as elegant, delicate, pure and sensitive.

Bigot's compositions, which include a set of Etudes and a *Rondeau*, are written in an early Romantic style using common Classical form. She was a sensitive and gifted composer.

Suite d'Etudes

    I.   Etude in C Minor - Allegro (2 ½ minutes)
    II.   Etude in A Minor - Allegretto (2 ½ minutes)

These etudes are from a set of six studies written in an early Romantic style.

Rate this piece: ☆☆☆☆☆

What I like about this piece (Etude in C Minor):	How I would describe this piece (Etude in C Minor):

What I like about this piece (Etude in A Minor):	How I would describe this piece (Etude in A Minor):

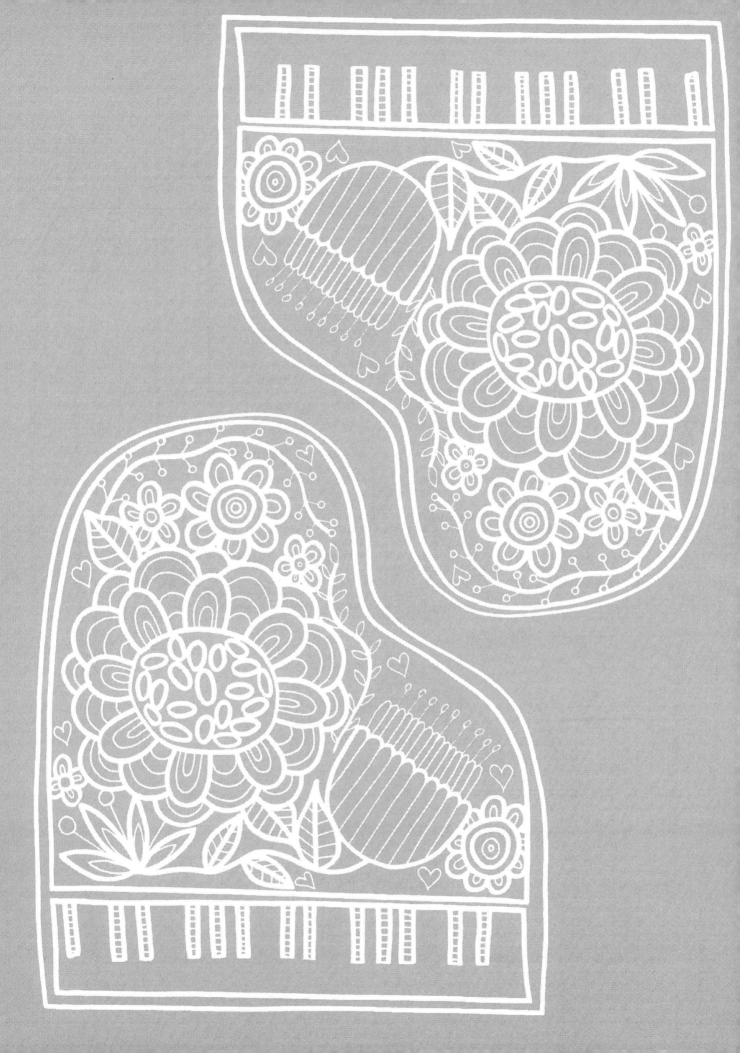

Maria Szymanowska

1789-1831
Poland

Maria Szymanowska was a Polish pianist, composer and piano teacher who had much in common with Frédéric Chopin, who was born twenty-one years later. She was a professional virtuoso pianist - one of the first in nineteenth-century Europe, and one of the first to perform memorized pieces in public. She made many concert tours, and she performed her own compositions as well as other works. Her playing was described as having a lyrical sense of virtuosity. She made the piano sing with an expressive, delicate tone.

Even before Chopin, she was the first to adapt Polish national dances like the **polonaise** and the **mazurka** to solo piano music. She wrote over one hundred compositions for solo piano. She composed in genres such as polonaises, mazurkas, nocturnes, waltzes, and preludes (just like Chopin would!) She was an important forerunner of Chopin, and Chopin was familiar with her music. She also wrote songs and some chamber works.

Like Chopin, Maria moved to Paris. She divorced her husband because he did not approve of her performing career. She was able to support herself and her three children by performing, teaching and composing.

Maria eventually ended up moving to St. Petersburg, Russia, where she was the court pianist to the Tsar of Russia. She toured all over Europe to places like Germany, France, Italy, England, Poland, Belgium, Holland and Austria.

Several composers dedicated pieces to her, including Johann Nepomuk Hummel and John Field. **Goethe** fell madly in love with her. She ran a **salon** in St. Petersburg that became a hub of cultural life and was visited by the Schumanns, Beethoven, Liszt, Chopin and many more famous composers.

Nocturne in B-Flat Major (4 minutes)

This beautiful nocturne is reminiscent of the nocturnes of **John Field**, who was a mentor to Szymanowska.

Rate this piece: ☆☆☆☆☆

What I like about this piece:	How I would describe this piece:

Prelude #2 (1 ½ minutes) Prelude #6 (3 minutes), Prelude #9 (1 ½ minutes)

Rate this piece: ☆☆☆☆☆

What I like about these pieces:	How I would describe these pieces:

18 Danses

Polonaise in F minor (3 minutes)
No. 7 Polonaise (5 minutes)

Rate this piece: ☆☆☆☆☆

What I like about these pieces:	How I would describe these pieces:

Mazurka No 12 (1 minute)

Szymanowska's mazurkas are charming and short works that are based on popular Polish folk material.

Rate this piece: ★☆☆☆☆

What I like about this piece:	How I would describe this piece:

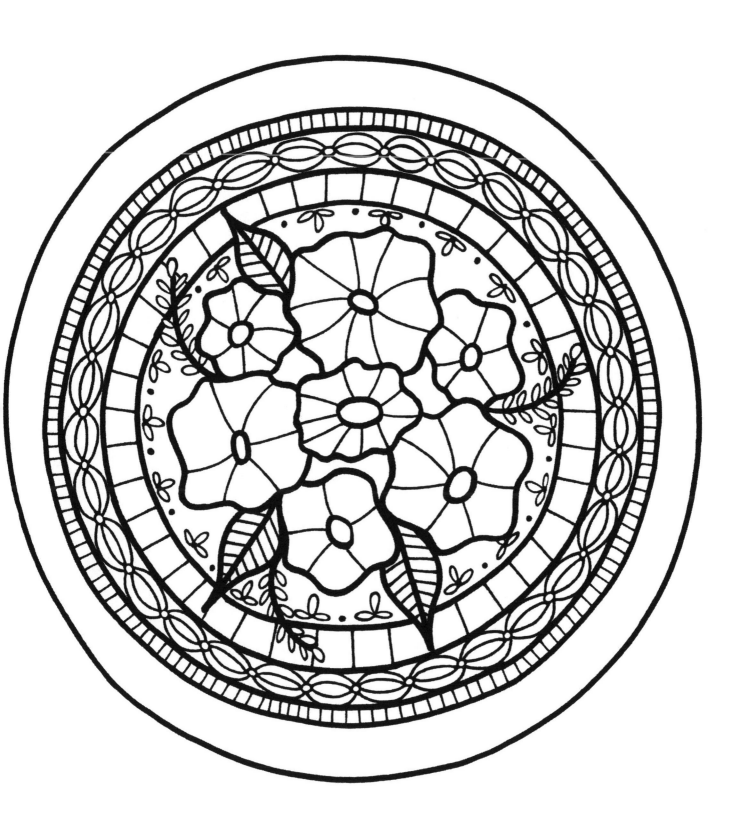

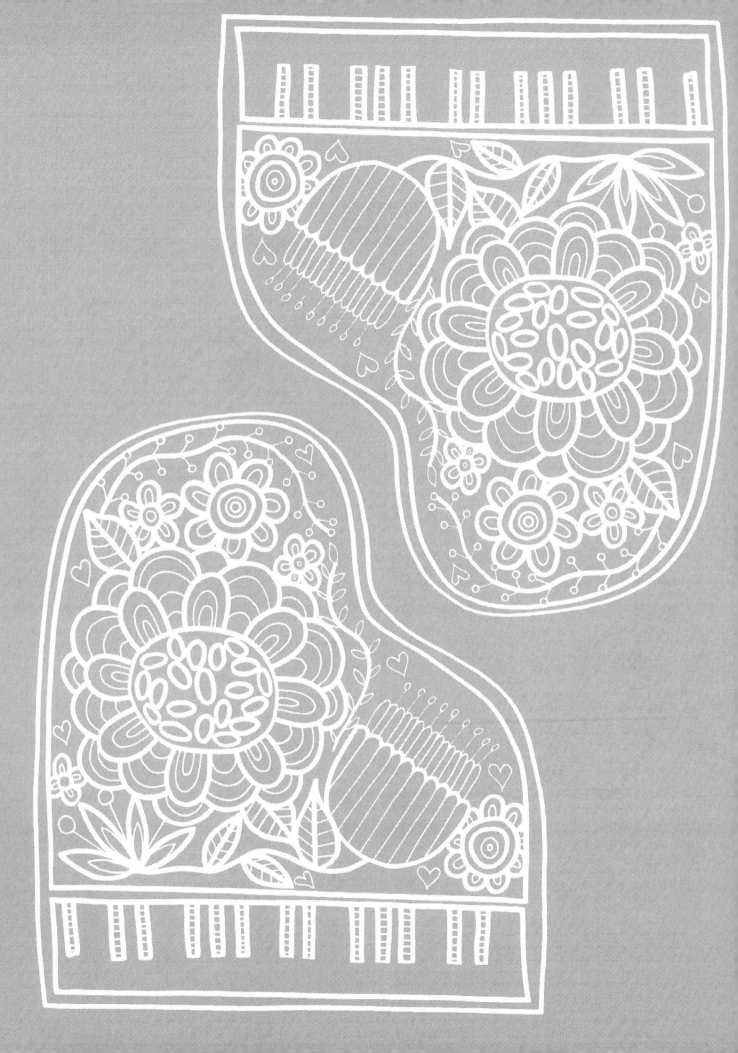

Louise Farrenc

1804-1875
France

Louise Farrenc was a brilliant performer, a prolific composer, a revered teacher and a music scholar. She was professor of piano at the Paris Conservatory for thirty years, holding the position at the prestigious conservatory longer than any other woman.

Louise was born in Paris to a family of royal painters and artists. She started her piano study at age six and at age fifteen entered the Paris Conservatory. She married Aristide Farrenc, an amateur **flautist** (they played concerts together) and a music publisher (he published her piano works), and they had one daughter, Victorine, who was her prize piano pupil.

She wrote many works for solo piano, but also composed in larger genres such as symphonies (she wrote three), symphonic overtures, piano trios and piano quintets. Her compositional style is Classical in form and genre, yet Romantic in harmonic language and range of musical expression. Her works were not only published during her lifetime, but were also widely performed and reviewed. After being paid less than the male teachers at the conservatory for many years, one of her compositions, her *Nonetto* op. 38 brought her so much publicity that she finally demanded and received equal pay.

In 1861 she was the first winner of a prestigious award for chamber music composition (the Prix Chartier Academie des Beaux-Arts); other later winners of the award included Gabriel Faure and Cesar Franck. Louise won the award again in 1869.

As a music scholar she published a huge twenty-three volume anthology of seventeenth- and eighteenth-century music.

Thirty Etudes in all Major and Minor Keys Op. 26

No. 10 in F sharp Minor (4 ½ minutes)
No. 17 in E flat Minor (1 ½ minutes)
No. 18 in D flat Major (3 minutes)

A music critic predicted that Farrenc's Thirty Etudes would become a piano classic. While Louise taught at the Paris Conservatory, her set of thirty etudes was adopted by the Conservatory as required piano repertoire for all piano students.

Rate this piece: ☆☆☆☆☆

What I like about these pieces:

How I would describe this piece (Etude in F sharp Minor):

How I would describe this piece (Etude in E flat Minor):

How I would describe this piece (Etude in D flat Major):

Air russe varie Op. 17 (12 minutes)

Robert Schumann praised this work, saying that it was "so sure in outline, so logical in development…that one must fall under their [the variations'] charm, especially since a subtle aroma of romanticism hovers over them."

Rate this piece: ☆ ☆ ☆ ☆ ☆

What I like about this piece:

How I would describe this piece:

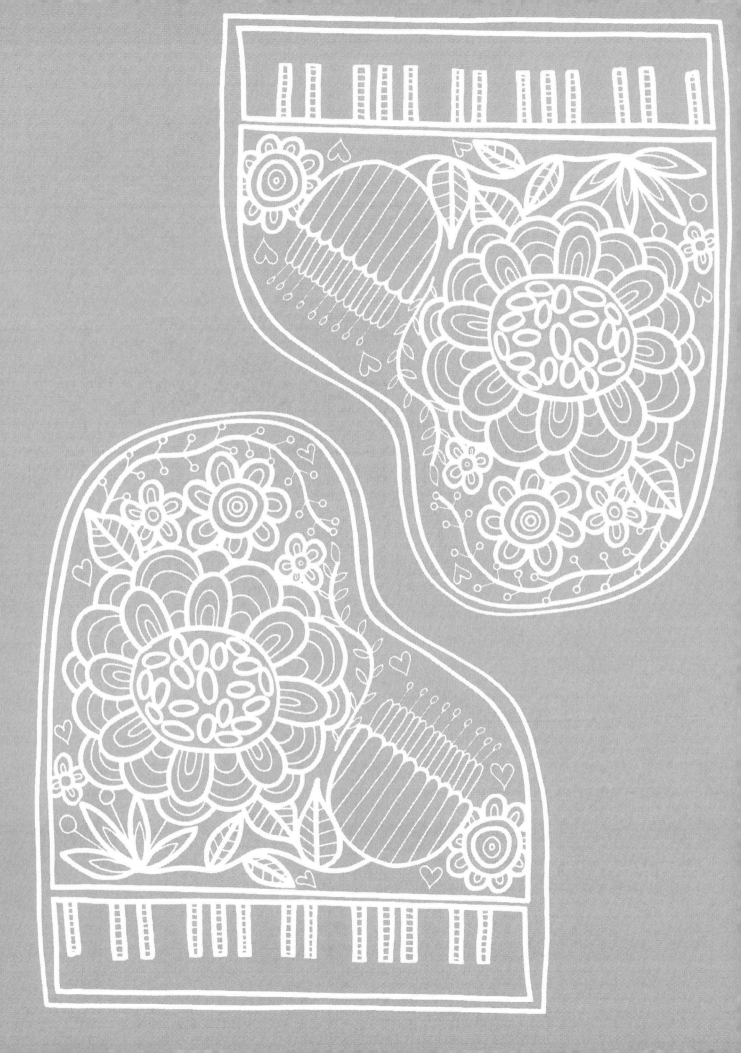

Fanny Mendelssohn Hensel

1805-1847
Germany

Fanny Mendelssohn Hensel, older sister of famous composer Felix Mendelssohn, was a highly gifted composer and pianist in her own right, but because of cultural expectations for women in her day she was not allowed to pursue music publicly. Therefore, her works are sadly not very well-known today. However, she left a large body of compositions, mainly songs and small piano works, but also some chamber, choral and orchestral works.

Fanny was extraordinarily talented. She had perfect pitch. She could perform all twenty-four Bach Preludes from the Well-Tempered Clavier from memory by age thirteen, and by age nineteen she had composed over thirty-two fugues. She had a love of early music and Beethoven (her only child, a son, was named Sebastian Ludwig Felix, after Bach, Beethoven, and her brother Felix). Her mother wrote that Fanny was "musical through and through." It was ironically through the female line in her family that she inherited her musical abilities: her great-aunt Sara Levy was a great harpsichordist who studied with one of the sons of Johann Sebastian Bach. Her mother, Lea Solomon Mendelssohn, was a brilliant pianist who was the first piano teacher of Fanny and Felix. Lea's piano teacher studied with Bach himself.

Fanny and Felix were very, very close. They relied on each other very much as they composed their music. They received the same training, studied with the same teachers and were both extremely talented. Their father, Abraham Mendelssohn, enjoyed and appreciated and encouraged Fanny in her musical training, however he did not approve of her going public with her music. Her compositions and performances would need to be confined to her home, where she was expected to focus on domestic responsibilities. So Felix went off to Europe to train, tour and immerse himself in great music, becoming one of the world's most well-known composers, while Fanny remained at home in the family's great mansion, *Leipzigerstrasse 3*, to fulfill her feminine duties.

As much as Felix loved and admired his sister, he and their father constantly discouraged her from publishing her compositions or in other ways going public with her music. She only had one public performance, which was performing Felix's Piano Concerto No. 1 for a benefit concert.

Fanny married Wilhelm Hensel, a painter. While the other men in Fanny's life discouraged her music in many ways, her husband was her champion in encouraging her in her composing. Because of social pressures, Fanny may have quit composing altogether when she got married. But Wilhelm pushed for her to compose, to make music and to publish her compositions. Each morning before he went to paint, he would leave a sheet of blank manuscript paper for her to encourage her to use her gift. She loved her domestic life and being a mother – she decided to forego hiring someone else to care for her son and to care for him herself. But there was always that desire to compose, to make music, to use her extraordinary talent.

The Mendelssohn women had a long-standing tradition of holding a weekly *Sonntagsmusiken*, or Sunday concert, in their home. This was the arena in which Fanny did most of her performing and for which she composed most of her music. Although not a real public and professional venue, these Sunday musical events drew good-sized crowds, including many leading musicians of the day. Fanny took over the planning of these events after the death of her mother and put much energy into creating these musical events of the highest quality.

Her husband Wilhelm and mother Lea continued to push for her to publish her music, but Fanny was hesitant for many years because Felix discouraged it so much. A few of her compositions had actually been published under her brother's name, but none under her own. She finally was brave enough to write to Felix and tell him that she was going to publish some of her music. Although he disagreed, he supported her. Publishing her music brought her great joy, and gave her a creative boost to continue to compose. After writing her Piano Trio (as a birthday present for her sister Rebecka), she wrote in her diary "I feel as if newly born." A year later, at the age of forty-one, Fanny died of a stroke.

Fanny Mendelssohn Hensel composed over 460 pieces of music in her short lifetime. Her compositional style is similar to her brother Felix's. One wonders what more she could have accomplished, what other great music would have come from her extraordinary talent, had she been allowed more opportunities like her brother.

Six melodies pour le piano, Op. 4 & 5

Andante soave in E-flat major (4 ½ minutes)

As you listen to this piece, listen for a simple, lyrical melody accompanied by beautiful rolling arpeggios.

Rate this piece: ☆☆☆☆☆

What I like about this piece:

How I would describe this piece:

Notturno in G Minor (6 minutes)

Much of Fanny Hensel's piano music can be described as *Lied ohne Worte*, or Songs Without Words. This is a genre that her brother Felix wrote much in and helped to popularize. Works in this genre are characterized by flowing lines and singing melodies. This Notturno (**Nocturne**) consists of a lilting melody over an arpeggiated accompaniment. Maurice Hinson calls this piece "one of Hensel's finest works."

Rate this piece: ☆☆☆☆☆

What I like about this piece:

How I would describe this piece:

Mendelssohn House in Berlin, where Fanny lived

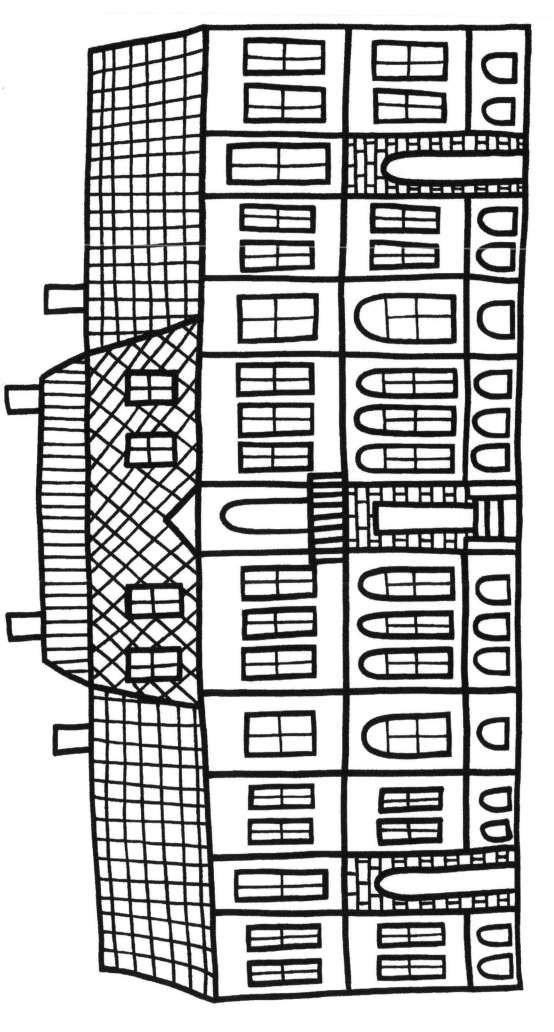

Piano Sonata in G Minor

II.   Scherzo (3 minutes)

The sonata was a musical genre that was customarily "off-limits" to female composers of Fanny's day. It was a big deal for anyone (let alone a woman) to write a sonata in the wake of Beethoven's masterpieces. By composing this piece she may have been testing her limits of the boundary between private and public music. This second movement of the G minor sonata is a shimmering **scherzo**, written in rondo form.

Rate this piece: ☆ ☆ ☆ ☆ ☆

What I like about this piece:	How I would describe this piece:

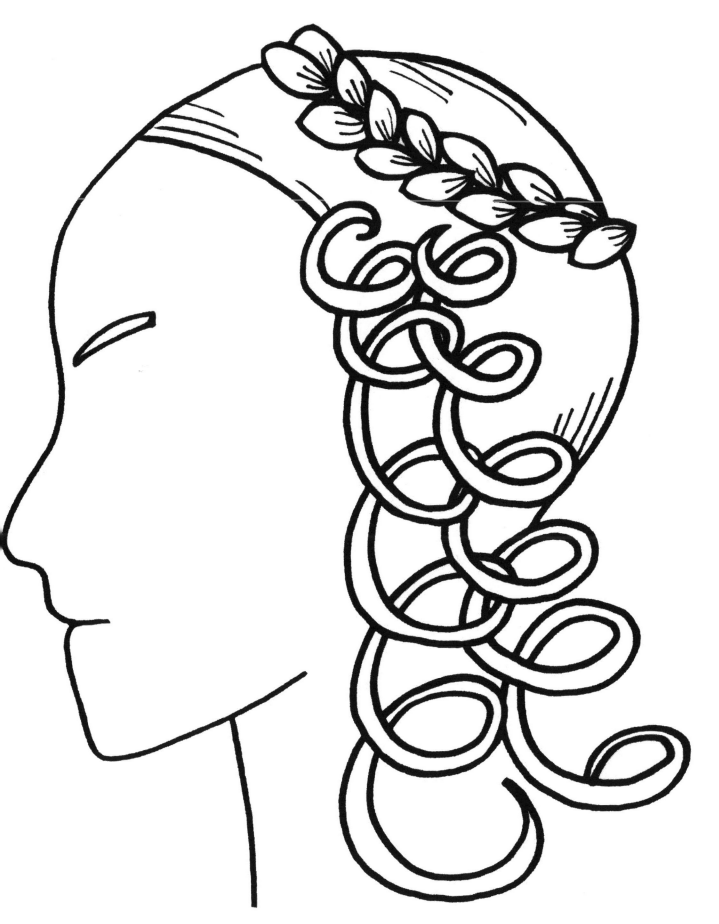

Easter Sonata in A Major (25 minutes)

I.   Allegro assai moderato
II.   Largo e molto espressivo – Poco piu mosso
III.   Allegretto – Scherzo
IV.   Allegro con strepito

This sonata was lost for 150 years. When it resurfaced in 1970 it was mistakenly attributed to Fanny's brother, Felix Mendelssohn. It wasn't until 2010 that Fanny was rightly given credit for composing this masterpiece.

Rate this piece: ☆☆☆☆☆

Movement 1: What I like about it, how I would describe it

Movement 2: What I like about it, how I would describe it

Movement 3: What I like about it, how I would describe it

Movement 4: What I like about it, how I would describe it

Piano Trio in D minor, Op. 11 (26 minutes)

I.   Allegro molto vivace
II.   Andante espressivo
III.   Lied: Allegretto
IV.   Finale: Allegretto moderato

This ambitious work was written during the year after Fanny finally told her brother that she was going to publish her music. It had been a creative and prolific year for her. This Piano Trio was written as a birthday gift for her sister Rebecka and was not published until three years after Fanny's death. It is a gorgeous, sweeping masterpiece with an interesting piano part. During the time she was composing this piece, Fanny wrote in her diary, "I feel as if newly born."

Rate this piece: ☆☆☆☆☆

Movement 1: What I like about it, how I would describe it	Movement 2: What I like about it, how I would describe it
Movement 3: What I like about it, how I would describe it	Movement 4: What I like about it, how I would describe it

6 Lieder, Op. 7

No. 1. *Nachtwanderer* (*Night wanderer*) (2 minutes)

Fanny had an impressive talent for songwriting and made a significant contribution to German **lieder**, composing over 250 songs in that genre.

Rate this piece: ★★★★★

What I like about this piece:	How I would describe this piece:

No. 6. *Dein ist mein Herz* (*Thine is my heart*) (2 minutes)

Rate this piece: ★★★★★

What I like about this piece:	How I would describe this piece:

Das Jahr

No. 2, February (3 minutes)

This impressive work, translated to "The Year," was inspired by a year the Hensels spent in Rome. It includes twelve character pieces, one for each month of the year, and a Postlude. The entire work is almost an hour in length, and Fanny's biographer calls it "one of the greatest of the unheralded piano suites of the nineteenth century." The second movement, "February," is a lilting, exuberant perpetual motion scherzo representing the Roman Carnival.

Rate this piece: ★ ☆ ☆ ☆ ☆

What I like about this piece:

How I would describe this piece:

Clara Wieck Schumann

1819-1896
Germany

Clara Schumann is one of the most well-known female composers. Hers is the most famous love story in all of classical music with her husband and great composer Robert Schumann. She lived an interesting life, full of much sadness, and had very complex relationships with the men in her life. She lived a lot of her musical life in the spotlight as a great concert pianist who toured all over Europe. She saw herself first as a performer, second as a mother (she and Robert had eight children), and third as a composer.

Clara was a melancholy child who didn't speak for the first four years of her life. Before she turned five her mother divorced her father, and because of the law she was put in the custody of her father. Her father, Friedrich Wieck, was a well-known music teacher who used his daughter as an example of his great teaching methods. He taught her piano, theory, harmony, counterpoint, composition, singing and violin. He was very demanding and controlling. He worked hard to get her performance opportunities and a lot of publicity. He was her first and only teacher, beginning at the age of four. She had her first official concert at age nine and started composing around the same time. She had her first extended concert tour when she was twelve or thirteen years old.

As a pianist she was a powerhouse. She had a large reach (she could reach a tenth) and played with great force and clarity. She was a child prodigy and a virtuoso. She was very popular as a performer – at one concert the police had to be there to control the crowd. She often had up to thirteen **curtain calls** and several **encores**. Her father trained her for this kind of life. He wanted his daughter in the limelight, perhaps because it was proof of his great teaching expertise. He trained her to perform despite anything that might be happening in life – chaos, illness, tragedy – Clara was able to play on. It was customary for performers of her day to play their own compositions, so Clara composed.

Young Robert Schumann became a piano student of Friedrich Wieck and moved in to their home when Clara was a child. They became friends, and then when she was a teenager they fell in love. He kissed her after her sixteenth birthday party. They wanted to marry but her father vehemently opposed the marriage. Finally, after a long legal battle, they married in 1840.

Clara was a great inspiration to Robert, and really was influential to his musical success. He, however, was not very encouraging to her in her composition. He believed that "men stand higher than women," and frequently made her feel very insecure about her compositions. His comments about her music must have really gotten to her, as she once tragically wrote, "I once believed I had creative talent, but I have given up this idea; a woman must not wish to compose."

While Clara lived for the spotlight of performing, Robert believed that the greatest artistry was achieved away from the public eye. He did not want his wife to perform publicly, but she loved it too much. He monopolized their piano for his composing, leaving little time for her to compose or even to practice. In the summer of 1853, when they finally lived somewhere with room for all of their children and both of their pianos, Clara said, "When I can work regularly I feel once more really in my element. A quite different feeling comes over me, lighter and freer and everything seems to become brighter and cheerful. Music is a large part of my life, and when I must do without it, it is as if I were deprived of bodily and mental vigour."

Clara continued to perform, going on several extended tours in-between the births of their eight children. Her husband Robert suffered from mental illness, and eventually ended up in an asylum until his death in 1856. Once he died, Clara stopped composing. She continued to perform to support her family, and in her sixties she was the principal piano instructor at a conservatory in Frankfurt, Germany.

A large portion of Clara's compositions are works for solo piano, however she also was a major contributor to German lieder, writing several songs based on poetry. Maurice Hinson said that "her piano works display a variety of emotions including enthusiasm, melancholy, passion, and sometimes sparkle."

Scherzo in D Minor, Op. 10 (5 minutes)

Clara's Scherzo Op. 10 was written during her youth, when she wrote a lot of big virtuoso works to show off her technical abilities. In this piece her large reach of a tenth comes in handy! This piece is one of her favorites of her own works, and it was also popular with audiences in Paris. Maurice Hinson calls it "a great dramatic display piece with two contrasting trios."

Rate this piece: ★☆☆☆☆

What I like about this piece:	How I would describe this piece:

Deuxieme scherzo in C Minor, Op. 14 (4 ½ minutes)

Rate this piece: ★☆☆☆☆

What I like about this piece:	How I would describe this piece:

Piano Concerto in A Minor, Op. 7

III.   Finale: Allegro non troppo – Allegro molto (11 minutes)

This was another work written during Clara's adolescence, beginning when she was just thirteen years old! She first performed her piano **concerto** when she was sixteen. (Felix Mendelssohn was the conductor for the premiere of this concerto!) It is a powerful and dramatic work, meant to show off her virtuosic abilities.

Rate this piece: ☆☆☆☆☆

What I like about this piece:

How I would describe this piece:

Piano Trio in G Minor, Op. 17 (28 minutes)

I. Allegro moderato
II. Scherzo and Trio
III. Andante
IV. Allegretto

For many, this piano trio is Clara's greatest achievement. It contains a lot of **contrapuntal** surprises and wit, and shows a mastery of sonata form. It was composed in 1846 during a very hard year for Clara, during which she suffered a miscarriage and lost her sixteen-month-old son. Her husband Robert wrote his own piano trio shortly after she wrote hers, after which she began to doubt the merit of her own piano trio.

Rate this piece: ★★★★☆

Movement 1: What I like about it, how I would describe it

Movement 2: What I like about it, how I would describe it

Movement 3: What I like about it, how I would describe it

Movement 4: What I like about it, how I would describe it

Variations on a Theme of Robert Schumann, Op. 20

(9 minutes)

Written for Robert's birthday a year before his nervous breakdown, this imaginative work is considered by some to be Clara's best work. Johannes Brahms also wrote a set of variations on this same theme.

Rate this piece: ☆ ☆ ☆ ☆ ☆

What I like about this piece:

How I would describe this piece:

Cecile Chaminade

1857-1944
France

Cecile Chaminade was a French pianist and composer who was very prolific and well-known during her day. She was one of the first women to make an actual career out of composing. She wrote over four hundred works in a wide variety of genres, the majority of them being songs (one hundred and thirty-five) and piano pieces (over two hundred). Almost all of her works were published during her lifetime, and they sold very well. Her music was especially popular in America.

Her compositions are typically referred to as charming "salon pieces," or music meant for performance as light entertainment in salons and homes. However, she actually did compose quite a few larger works in more "serious" genres, such as concerti, orchestral suites, a ballet, an opera, chamber music and a choral symphony. Her larger piano works include a piano sonata, two sets of concert etudes, six pieces for piano and orchestra and a concerto, or *Concertstuck,* for piano and orchestra.

Cecile Chaminade was born in Paris to a family of amateur musicians. Her mother was her first piano teacher. Apparently she was able to meet some important figures in French music, for she played for Georges Bizet (who was her neighbor) as a young girl, and Hector Berlioz convinced Cecile's parents that they should seek out the best possible musical instruction for their daughter. It is even rumored that she may have played for and impressed the great Franz Liszt.

Because her father forbade her enrollment at the Paris Conservatory, Cecile studied privately with professors from the conservatory. She began writing her own compositions at age eight, and had her Parisian piano debut at age eighteen. She then toured England and France. In 1908 she had her American debut.

Chaminade's music is tuneful and elegant, and often witty. She garnered so much popularity in America that a national group of music clubs was named after her.

Composer Ambroise Thomas said of her, "This is not a woman who composes, but a composer who is a woman."

Piano Sonata in C Minor, Op. 21

I.   Allegro appassionato (7 minutes)

Chaminade dedicated this, her only piano sonata, to composer Moritz Moszkowski (who was her brother-in-law!). The first movement has passion and drama, and includes a fugue-like section in the middle.

Rate this piece: ☆☆☆☆☆

What I like about this piece:	How I would describe this piece:

Scarf Dance (2 ½ minutes)

This piece came from a movement of the only ballet Chaminade wrote. She arranged it for piano and it became one of her most famous pieces.

Rate this piece: ★ ☆ ☆ ☆ ☆

What I like about this piece:	How I would describe this piece:

6 Etudes de concert, Op. 35

No. 1: Scherzo. Allegro (3 minutes)

This scherzo is in the key of C major. It is a study in the rapid contrast between staccato and legato. Hinson says that these concert etudes have "impressive scale and imagination."

Rate this piece: ☆ ☆ ☆ ☆ ☆

What I like about this piece:	How I would describe this piece:

No. 2: Automne. Lento (7 minutes)

This etude has a beautiful melody in the middle of the piano, supported by resonant harmonies. The middle section moves and becomes more passionate and virtuosic.

Rate this piece: ☆ ☆ ☆ ☆ ☆

What I like about this piece:	How I would describe this piece:

Concertstuck (16 minutes)

Chaminade premiered this work for piano and orchestra in 1888. It was performed many times in Paris, London, and America. In composing this work Chaminade was influenced by Wagner and Liszt, as well as French composers Saint-Saens and Bizet.

Rate this piece: ☆ ☆ ☆ ☆ ☆

What I like about this piece:	How I would describe this piece:

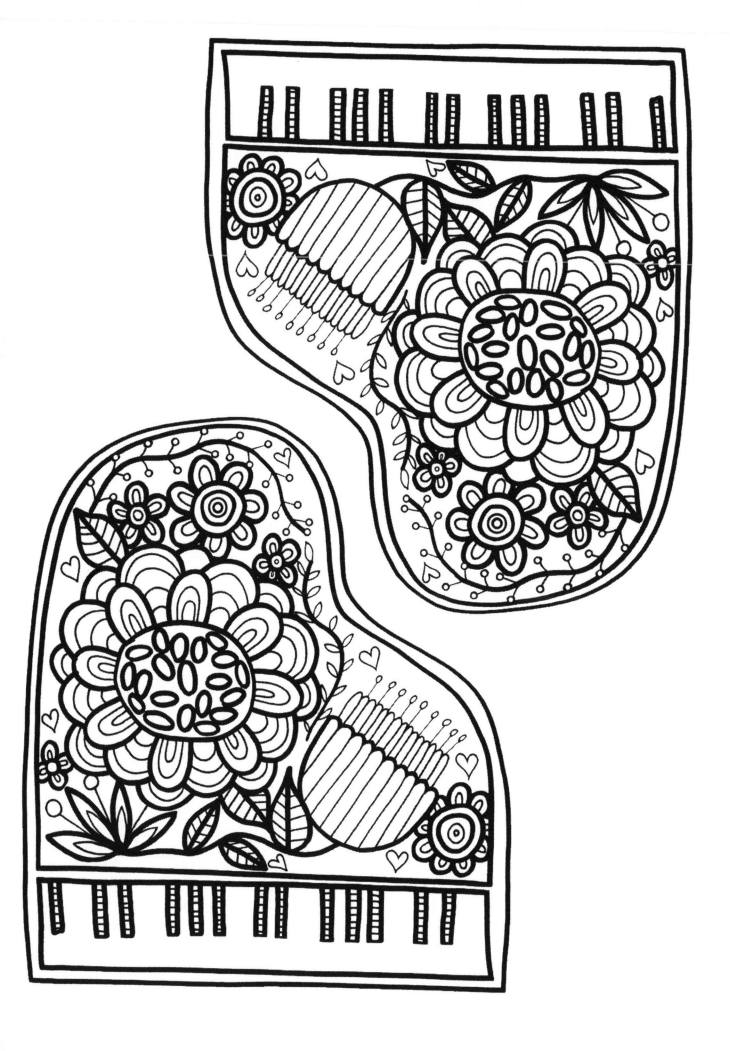

Amy Beach

1867-1944
United States

Amy Beach was an American composer of the early
twentieth century who was fortunate to be able to focus
on composing for her whole life. She earned a lot of
respect and enjoyed popularity during her lifetime, was able to
have most of her works published, and helped to pave the way
for other women composers to have large compositions
performed by major orchestras. Beach is perhaps the greatest
American woman composer.

Amy was a child prodigy. Her mother, Clara, a pianist and
singer, noticed eighteen-month-old Amy harmonizing with her bedtime lullabies and
knew her daughter was gifted. Young Amy heard music in colors and would cry for the
"pink" music (music in the key of E-flat) to be played. Each key was a different color to
Amy!

At age four, Amy was composing simple pieces at the piano, and at age six she began
formal piano lessons with her mother. Her first public performance was at age seven. As a
teenager she soloed with the Boston Symphony. At age eighteen she married forty-three-
year-old Dr. Henry Harris Aubrey Beach, a well-known surgeon, whom she met when
he treated her sore finger. He was an amateur musician.

Once she was married, her husband only allowed her to perform publicly once or twice a
year, although he did encourage her composing. So she concentrated on composition and
was very prolific. She essentially composed for the rest of her life. Because they never had
children, her music was her main focus throughout her life. Because of her husband's
financial support, she also never had to teach to support herself.

Amy differed from a lot of other composers of her time, in that she never studied in
Europe and she never formally studied composition, except for a few years of harmony

studies as a teenager. She was basically self-taught in composition – in fact, she taught herself counterpoint by writing down (from memory!) much of Bach's *Well-Tempered Clavier.*

Amy was one of the first American women to have large genre compositions (such as symphony, concerto and mass) performed widely by major orchestras. Her works were not only performed in the United States but also abroad. She wrote one symphony, her *Gaelic* Symphony, as well as an opera, a mass, a piano concerto and several works for chorus and orchestra. She also wrote several works for chamber ensembles, such as a string quartet and a piano trio, and many piano pieces and many songs. Her songs are some of her most popular works.

After 25 years of marriage, her husband died and Amy resumed her performing career. She moved to Europe, where she lived and toured for several years. She continued to compose into her seventies.

Amy's musical influences include Wagner, Brahms and Debussy, as well as fellow-American composer Edward MacDowell. Her style has reflections of each of these composers' music and includes lots of complex harmonies and lush **chromaticism**. It has been said that she possessed a natural gift for melody, which is evident in her songs. Maurice Hinson describes her music in this way: "The forward-moving drive throughout Beach's writing seems to be the essence of early twentieth-century optimism."

Amy Beach stated in 1915 that she had never felt limited because she was a woman.

Symphony in E Minor, Op. 32, *Gaelic*

I. Allegro con fuoco (12 minutes)

II. Alla Siciliana – Allegro Vivace – Andante (8 minutes)

This is the first symphony ever to be composed and published by a female American composer. It has four contrasting movements. Listen to the first two movements of this symphony. The exciting first movement, "Allegro Con Fuoco" (meaning "quick, with fire") sets the stage for this Romantic symphony. The beautiful and lyrical second movement introduces the Gaelic themes using variation.

Rate this piece: ☆☆☆☆☆

What I like about this piece (Allegro con fuoco):

How I would describe this piece (Allegro con fuoco):

What I like about this piece (Alla Siciliana):

How I would describe this piece (Alla Siciliana):

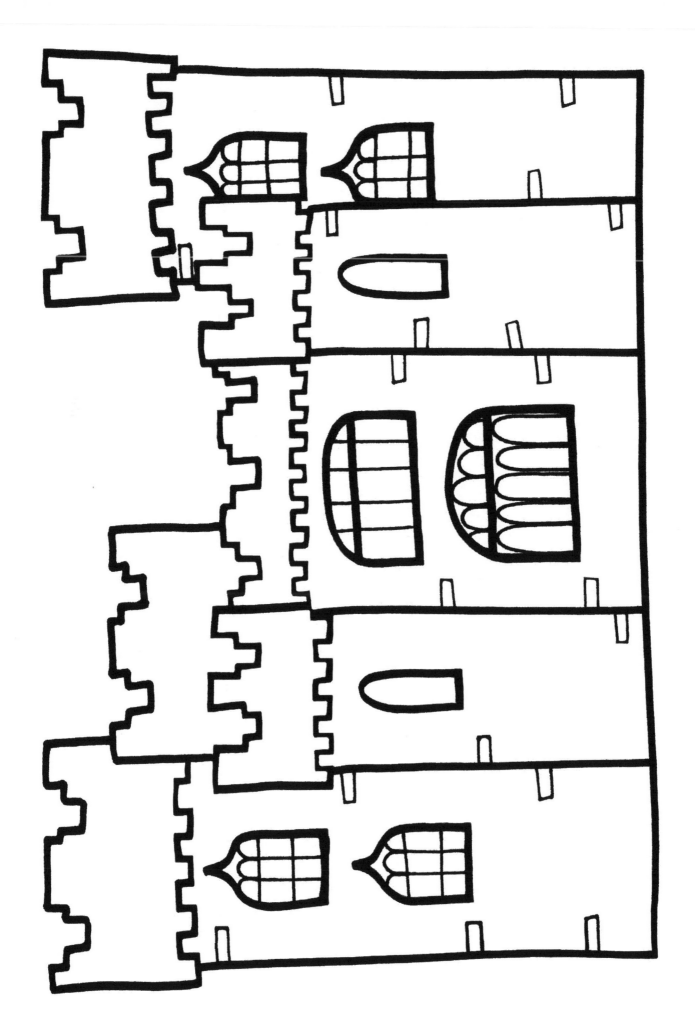

Quartet for Strings in One Movement, Op. 89 (13 minutes)

This beautiful work for string quartet is very original and lyrical. It is tunefully crafted, with many gorgeous moments. She based some of this work off of Alaska Inuit melodies. This work is highly chromatic and has some impressionistic qualities.

Rate this piece: ☆☆☆☆☆

What I like about this piece:

How I would describe this piece:

Eskimos, Four Characteristic Pieces, Op. 64

    I.   Arctic Night (3 minutes)
    II.   The Returning Hunter (1 minute)
    III.   Exiles (3 minutes)
    IV.   With Dog-Teams (2 minutes)

This four-piece suite was written for children but exhibits some wonderful and quite original writing. Beach based this suite off of several Alaskan Inuit tunes, adding beautiful harmonies to bring them to life on the piano.

Rate this piece: ☆ ☆ ☆ ☆ ☆

Arctic Night: What I like about it, how I would describe it	The Returning Hunter: What I like about it, how I would describe it
Exiles: What I like about it, how I would describe it	With Dog-Teams: What I like about it, how I would describe it

Four Sketches Op. 15
III. Dreaming (6 minutes)

This gorgeous piece is very Romantic in style and is reminiscent of Liszt.

Rate this piece: ☆☆☆☆☆

What I like about this piece:	How I would describe this piece:

IV. Fire-flies (3 ½ minutes)

Full of charm, this piece depicts fireflies fluttering through the night sky. It is quite an impressive technical study involving lots of very quick thirds in the right hand.

Rate this piece: ☆☆☆☆☆

What I like about this piece:	How I would describe this piece:

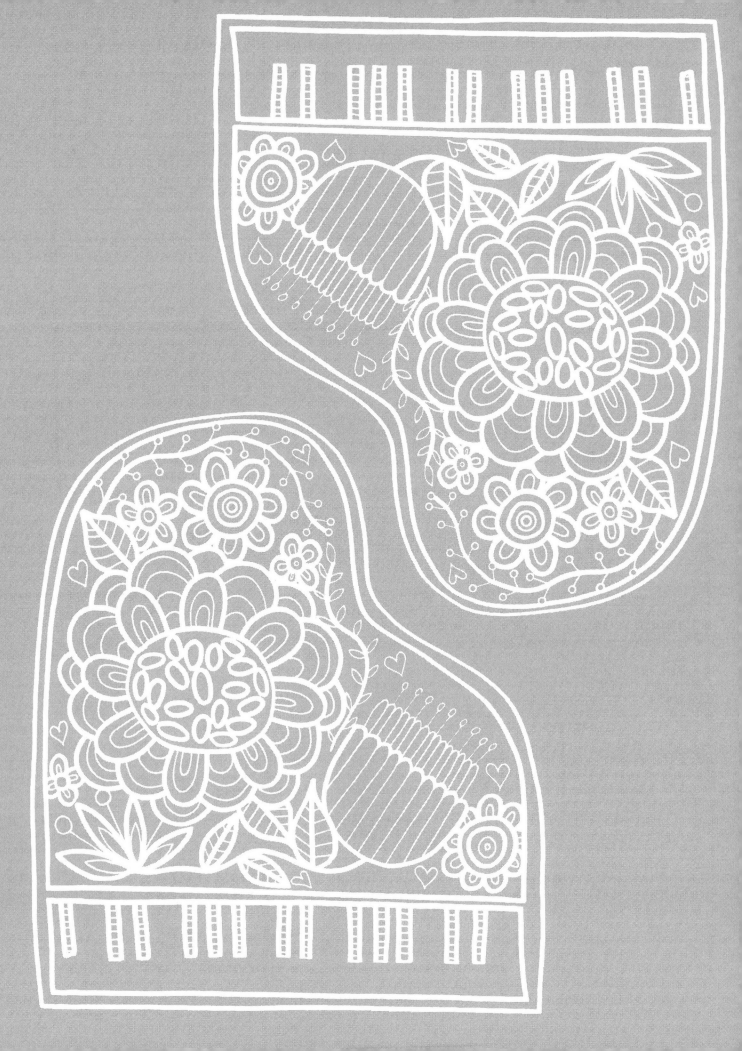

From Grandmother's Garden Op. 97

I.   "Morning Glories" (1 ½ minutes)

This short shimmering piece is fast and charming.

Rate this piece: ★★★★★

What I like about this piece:	How I would describe this piece:

V.   "Honeysuckle" (3 minutes)

This fast-paced piece includes some great chromatic harmonies.

Rate this piece: ★★★★★

What I like about this piece:	How I would describe this piece:

Chanson d'amour (4 ½ minutes)

Amy Beach's songs were among some of her most famous works during her lifetime.

Rate this piece: ☆ ☆ ☆ ☆ ☆

What I like about this piece:	How I would describe this piece:

Rebecca Clarke

1886-1979
England

Rebecca Clarke was an English composer and viola player. She was one of the most distinguished British women composers of her day, as well as one of the foremost violists and chamber artists. She performed chamber music with many of the greatest performers of her day.

The daughter of an American father and a British mother, Rebecca began playing the violin at age eight. She later studied at the Royal Academy of Music and the Royal College of Music in London, being the first female to study composition under Charles Stanford. It was Stanford who suggested that she switch from violin to viola.

After composing her famous Viola Sonata, she entered it in a composition competition sponsored by Elizabeth Sprague Coolidge (an American pianist and music patron). Entries were submitted to the jury of six men without composers' names attached. The competition was down to the top two entries – Rebecca Clarke's Viola Sonata, and great composer Ernest Bloch's Viola Suite – and it was deadlocked at a tie. Mrs. Coolidge cast the tie-breaking vote. Clarke ended up winning second place, but Mrs. Coolidge later wrote, "You should have seen the faces of the jury when it was revealed the composer was a woman!"

Rebecca Clarke was among the first six female full members of a professional London orchestra. She was a member of three all-women chamber ensembles. She toured worldwide, and even performed at Carnegie Hall in 1918.

Rebecca moved back and forth between the United Kingdom and the United States, and then had to remain in the United States at the outbreak of World War II. She married old college friend and pianist James Friskin. She performed and composed little after marriage but continued to stay in the musical world by lecturing, teaching and promoting chamber music.

Clarke wrote close to one hundred works, but only twenty were published during her lifetime. Her works include songs, choral works, chamber works and a couple of pieces for solo piano (which are unpublished). Her musical influences include Debussy, Ravel, Scriabin and Bloch; she wrote with power and passion in a range of styles including Impressionism, post-Romantic and neo-Classical. By the time she passed away in 1979, all of her songs were out of print.

Viola Sonata (7 ½ minutes)

This is the piece that tied for first place with Ernest Bloch in the Coolidge competition. It was so unheard of for a woman to receive recognition for composing a piece of that caliber that Rebecca later said this about the competition:

> "And when I had that one little whiff of success that I've had in my life, with the Viola Sonata, the rumour went around, I hear, that I hadn't written the stuff myself, that somebody had done it for me. And I even got one or two little bits of press clippings saying that it was impossible, that I couldn't have written it myself. And the funniest of all was that I had a clipping once which said that I didn't exist, there wasn't any such person as Rebecca Clarke, that it was a pseudonym for Ernest Bloch!"

Rate this piece: ★ ☆ ☆ ☆ ☆

What I like about this piece:	How I would describe this piece:

I'll Bid My Heart Be Still (3 ½ minutes)

This gorgeous and simple setting of a Scottish tune was Clarke's last work for viola. She wrote this song for her husband James a few months before their marriage. After receiving this beautiful piece he encouraged her to compose more, although she never did.

Rate this piece: ★ ☆ ☆ ☆ ☆

What I like about this piece:	How I would describe this piece:

Lili Boulanger

1893-1918
France

Lili Boulanger was a fascinating composer who wrote some amazing music during her tragically short life. Lili grew up living a very cultured and privileged life. Her father was a composer who wrote operas and even had won the Prix de Rome (a prestigious French scholarship for the arts). Her mother was a Russian princess. Her older sister Nadia was also a well-known composer and composition teacher.

When Lili was two she had bronchial pneumonia, which weakened her immune system and resulted in her being very ill throughout her short life.

The Boulangers attended the theatre, concerts, the opera, and fancy dinners. They vacationed in the south of France. At age eighteen, Lili learned to ride a bicycle by taking cycling lessons and would go on long bike rides as her health would permit.

Because Boulanger was a woman she was not allowed to attend the Paris Conservatory, but she did study with some of the teachers, including the famous composer Gabriel Faure.

Boulanger was very determined, had a strong work ethic as her health allowed, and was somewhat of a rule-bender. Lili's sister Nadia had come very close to winning the Prix de Rome, but in the end did not win, probably because she was a woman. Lili was determined to win and began working hard on her musical compositions. In 1913 she became the first woman to win the Prix de Rome, which she won with a cantata called *Faust et Helene*. As a result of winning the Prix de Rome she also signed a music publishing contract with a publisher.

Tragically, Lili died in 1918 at the young age of twenty-five as a result of her poor health. Shortly before she died, she dictated her *Pie Jesu* from her bed. One can only imagine what great music she might have composed had she lived longer.

Lili Boulanger is best remembered for her choral music. She also wrote chamber music, one opera and a few instrumental works. She only wrote a handful of pieces for solo piano, but what she did write is profound and breathtaking. Her ability to compose was unquestionably hindered by her poor health, but when she was able to compose she wrote surely and quickly. She had great musical vision and wrote with advanced harmonic language and contrapuntal strength.

Theme and Variations (9 minutes)

This outstanding theme and variations takes a simple, haunting melody and weaves it into a poignant and evocative masterpiece. It is written in a late French Romantic style.

Rate this piece: ☆☆☆☆☆

What I like about this piece:

How I would describe this piece:

Trois Morceaux *(Three Pieces)*

D'un Vieux Jardin *(From an Old Garden)* (2 ½ minutes)
D'un Jardin Clair *(From a Bright Garden)* (2 minutes)
Cortège *(Procession)* (2 minutes)

These beautiful little pieces are quite impressionistic in style. Listen to the gorgeous harmonies and hear the scenes that they evoke.

Rate this piece: ★ ☆ ☆ ☆ ☆

What I like about this piece:

How I would describe this piece (D'un Vieux Jardin):

How I would describe this piece (D'un Jardin Clair):

How I would describe this piece (Cortege):

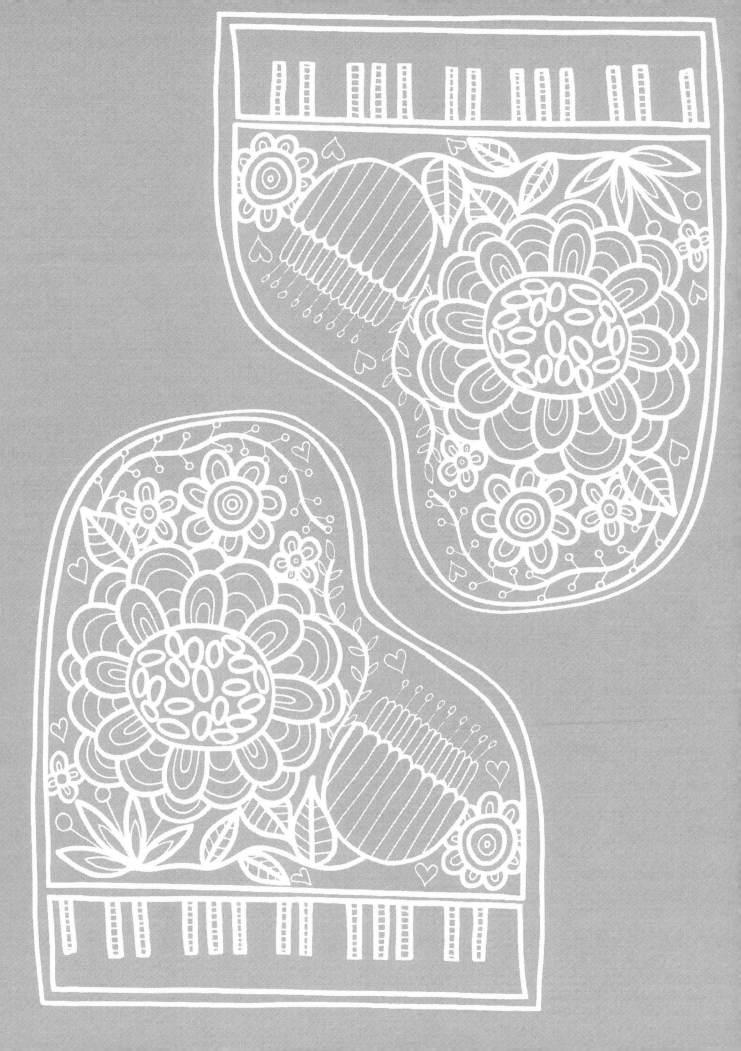

Judith Lang Zaimont

born 1945
United States

Judith Lang Zaimont is an internationally-recognized American composer who has had a remarkable career as a concertizing and recording pianist, composer, professor of music and lecturer. As a composer she has been very prolific, composing over one hundred works in genres such as orchestral (including four symphonies), chamber, choral, keyboard, vocal, opera and wind ensemble. She has written over twenty works (including solos, suites and a concerto) for solo piano, and they are outstanding. Many of her works are prize-winning and many have been recorded. In the words of the composer herself, "My music reaches both heart and mind." Her music has a distinctive style and "expressive strength."

Judith was born into a musical family. As a young child she began piano lessons with her mother, and began composing at age twelve. Throughout her teenage years she attended the Juilliard Preparatory School where she studied with Rosina Lhevinne. As a teenager and young adult she toured the United States with her sister Doris as a piano duo, performing at Carnegie Hall and appearing on television shows. Zaimont earned a Bachelor of Music degree, an Artist's Diplomat in Piano and a Masters degree in Music Composition. She received a MacDowell Fellowship to study at the MacDowell Colony, and a Debussy scholarship to study composition in Paris.

Zaimont says, "I admire the unusual – music that takes risks." She retired from teaching in 2005 and continues to compose full-time.

Serenade (6 ½ minutes)

This gorgeous, flowing piece has beautiful, fresh harmonies with a ringing, lyrical melody.

Rate this piece: ★ ☆ ☆ ☆ ☆

What I like about this piece:	How I would describe this piece:

Nocturne: La Fin de Siècle (Galaxy) (7 minutes)

This beautiful composition adds a modern flair to the traditional Romantic-style nocturne. Listen for a beautiful lyrical melody with a flowing accompaniment in the first and last section. The middle of the piece escalates into a whirlwind of dissonance, creating a strong contrast to the expressive nature of the beginning and ending sections.

Rate this piece: ★ ☆ ☆ ☆ ☆

What I like about this piece:	How I would describe this piece:

Sonata for Piano Solo

    I.   Ricerca (10 minutes)
   III.   Impronta digitale (8 minutes)

The opening movement, *Ricerca*, which could be translated to mean a "search" or a "quest," begins serenely with gorgeous, thoughtful chords, gradually adding dissonance upon dissonance and then spiraling into a syncopated stream of musical consciousness. This exploration continues until it finds its way to an enlightened ending with chords to echo the opening measures.

Movement three, *Impronta digitale*, meaning "fingerprint," is fast, relentless, dramatic and fierce and is a fitting virtuosic ending to the sonata.

Rate this piece: ☆ ☆ ☆ ☆ ☆

What I like about this piece (Ricerca):	How I would describe this piece (Ricerca):

What I like about this piece (Impronta digitale):	How I would describe this piece (Impronta digitale):

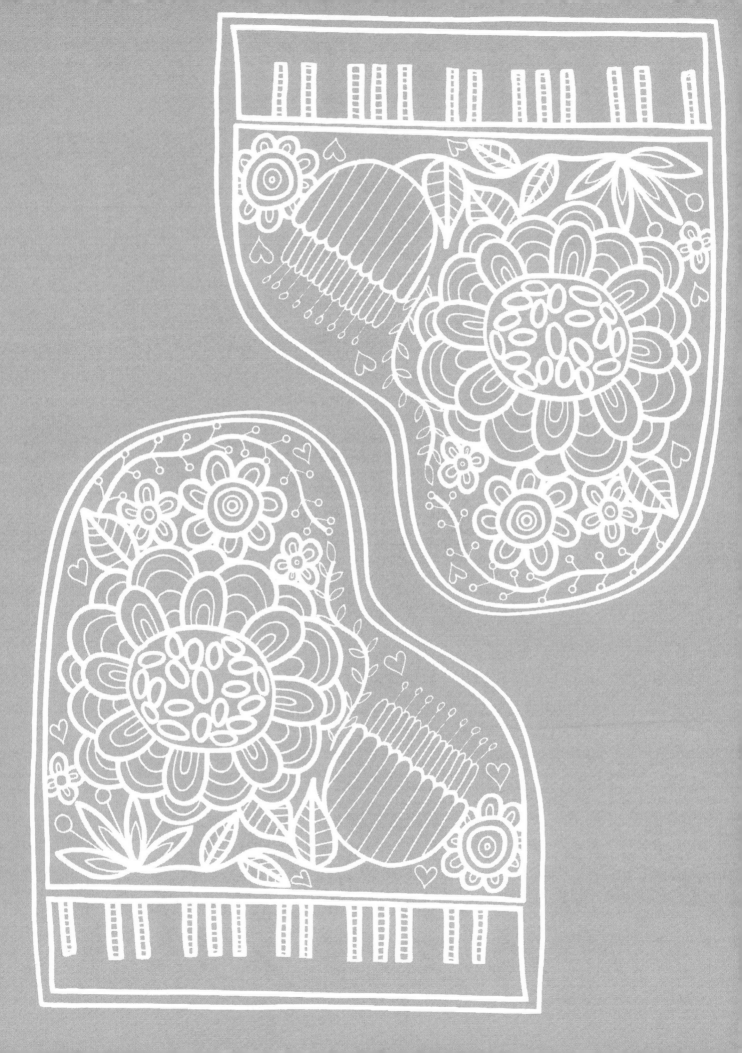

Alexina Louie

born 1949
Canada

Alexina Louie is a Canadian composer whose works have become a part of the standard repertoire. Her piano compositions in particular are popular amongst professionals and students. She has quite the eclectic range of influences in her music, including the Chinese culture and eastern/Oriental influences, poetry, her environmental concerns, visual arts and more.

Louie received a Bachelor of Music degree in Music History and a Master of Arts degree in Composition. She has won several awards, including the Canadian Music Council Composer of the Year in 1986, and the SOCAN Concert Music Award for the most performed Classical composer of the year in 1990, 1992 and 2003.

Alexina Louie is a prolific composer with several works in each of the genres of orchestral, orchestral with soloist, large ensemble, chamber ensemble, solo, opera, ballet, vocal and choral music. She has also composed TV and film scores and electronic music.

I Leap Through the Sky with Stars (8 minutes)

Written in 1991, this work for piano solo was written in memory of the great pianist Glenn Gould and Claude Vivier, a Canadian composer. It is based on a Zen poem. This colorful piece includes a lot of extremes in range and dynamics, changing meters, **consonance** and **dissonance**, and opposing white keys in one hand with black keys in the other. It was written using **pentatonic** and **whole-tone scales**.

Rate this piece: ☆☆☆☆☆

What I like about this piece:	How I would describe this piece:

In a Flash (5 ½ minutes)

Written in 2006, this piano solo has a lot of colorful harmonies, and begins with a rising four-note motive that is repeated again and again in a perpetual motion frenzy. Throughout the piece there are lots of fast scales juxtaposed with interesting harmonies. You can hear a definite impressionistic influence in this exciting piece.

Rate this piece: ★☆☆☆☆

What I like about this piece:	How I would describe this piece:

Music for Piano: Changes (2 ½ minutes)

This piece comes from a suite of four contemporary solo piano pieces. The pieces have a mystical sound to them. The other pieces in the suite are "The Enchanted Bells," "Distant Memories" and "Once Upon a Time."

Rate this piece: ☆☆☆☆☆

What I like about this piece:	How I would describe this piece:

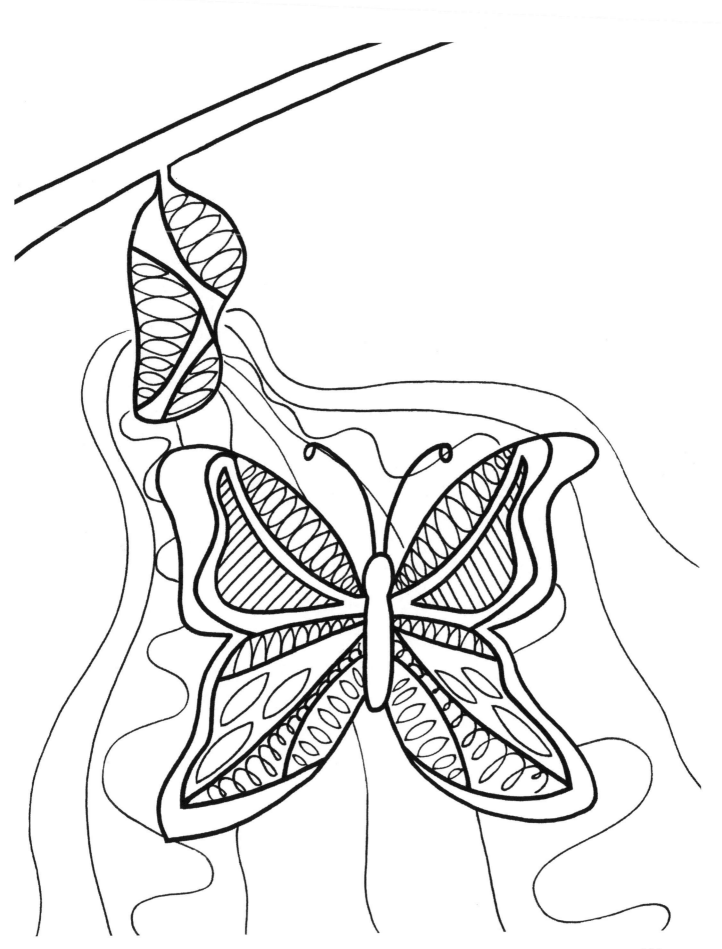

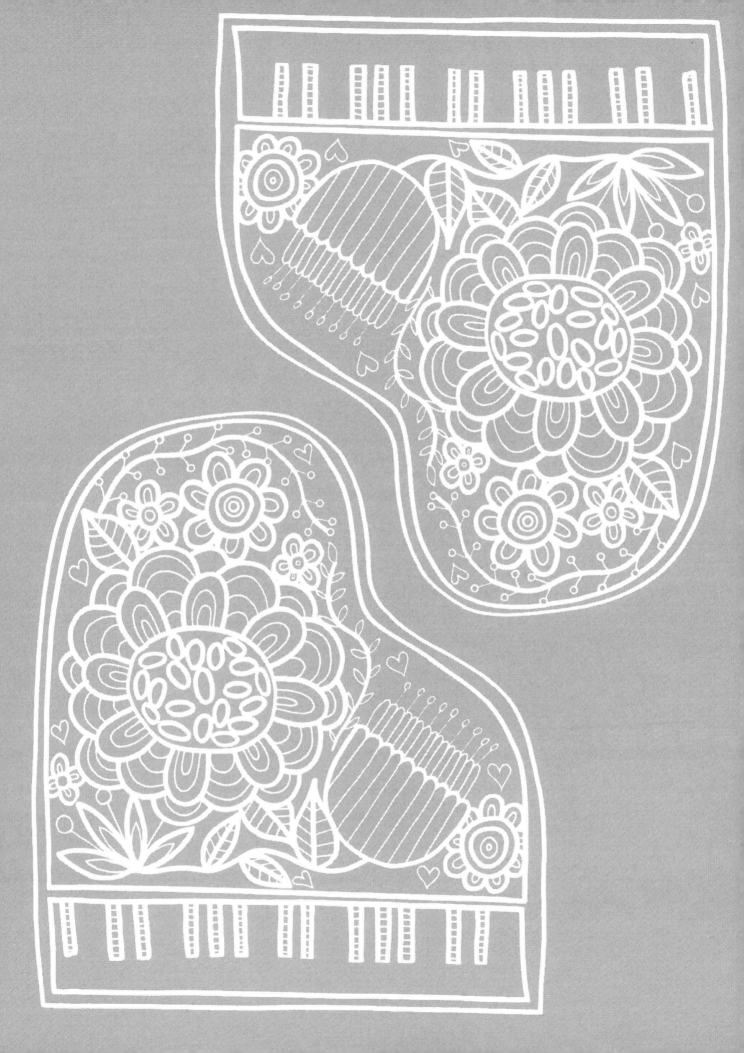

Cecilia McDowall

born 1951
United Kingdom

Cecilia McDowall is a British composer who has won many awards, including the British Composer Award in 2014 for choral music. Her compositions include orchestral, chamber, instrumental, vocal, choral, wind and brass works as well as works for the stage and several educational works, mostly for flute and piano.

From her biography on her website: "Cecilia McDowall has been described by the International Record Review as having 'a communicative gift that is very rare in modern music'. Often inspired by extra-musical influences, her writing combines a rhythmic vitality with expressive lyricism 'which is, at times, intensely moving'."

Colour is the Keyboard (5 ½ minutes)

Composed in 2007, this inventive piece focuses on synaesthesia, or the crossing over of the senses. Some synaesthetes associate sounds with specific colors. This work for solo piano is based on two famous synaesthetes – the painter Kandinsky (and more specifically his painting "Yellow-Red-Blue") and the composer Scriabin, who associated colors with all of the keys. McDowall uses Scriabin's key associations with the colors yellow, red, and blue (D, C, and F#) as the basis for this piece.

Kandinsky said this about color and music: "Color is the keyboard, the eyes are the hammers, the soul is the piano with many strings. The artist is the hand that plays, touching one key or another purposely, to cause vibrations in the soul."

Rate this piece: ☆ ☆ ☆ ☆ ☆

What I like about this piece:	How I would describe this piece:

Listening Selections | Cecilia McDowall

Four Piano Solos: Vespers in Venice (3 minutes)

McDowall got her inspiration for this piece from a painting. *Vespers in Venice* is based on J.M.W. Turner's 1844 painting *Approach to Venice*. The blurred texture of the piano writing reflects the misty haze of this painting, which depicts a scene with a cloudy sky going from golds to blues as the sun sets; the outline of Venice and St. Mark's Cathedral can be seen in the distance. You can also almost hear the opening fanfare of Monteverdi's *Vespers* and the bells of Venice in this piece.

Rate this piece: ☆ ☆ ☆ ☆ ☆

What I like about this piece:	How I would describe this piece:

St. Mark- s Cathedral, Venice

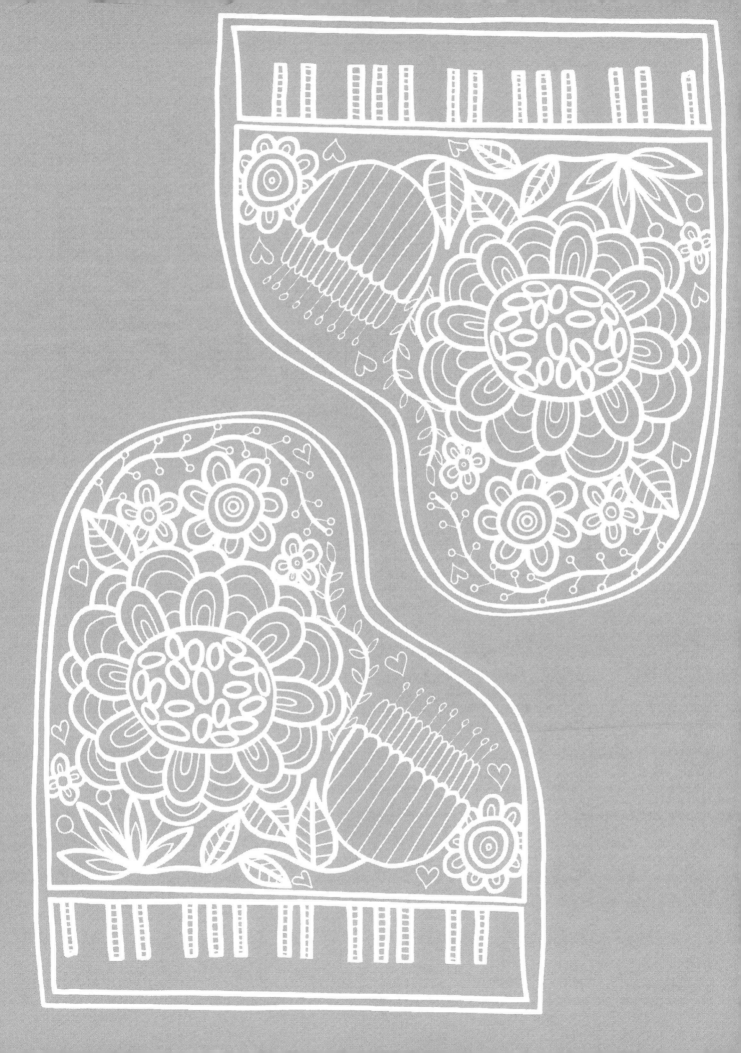

June Armstrong

born 1951
Ireland

June Armstrong is an Irish composer of educational piano music for young pianists. Her compositions focus on interpretation and atmospheric playing, tone and technical development. She writes music that will engage the imagination. As a composer she is inspired by her passion for piano teaching, which she discovered as she started teaching her two sons piano lessons over twenty-five years ago.

Armstrong's musical training began as a young child, when she learned to play the piano and the violin. She went on to study musical composition, earning a bachelor's and a master's degree at Queen's University Belfast. After teaching her two young sons piano she went on to earn her piano teaching diploma, then made a career out of teaching. June co-founded the European Piano Teachers' Association Belfast branch.

She currently has fifteen books of piano music published, each with finely-crafted original music in a variety of moods and styles, from elementary to advanced levels.

Armstrong loves playing the violin, playing Bach, walking and watching the sea.

Enchanted World (Excerpts, 10 minutes)

The Forest
The Little Black Cloud
Bursting the Balloon
The Spelling of Happy Birthday
Sing Ho!
Boggy and Sad
Look at Me Jumping
The Terrible Flood
Bedtime
A Very Busy Day
The Jugular Jaguar
In the Mist
A Very Blusterous Day
An Enchanted Place

This set of thirty short pieces is based on A.A. Milne's Winnie the Pooh. Full of wit and humor, the pieces are original and vividly evoke the Hundred Acre Wood and all its inhabitants. Winnie the Pooh and his friends come to life in these fun pieces for elementary-leveled pianists!

Rate this piece: ☆☆☆☆☆

What I like about this piece:

How I would describe this piece:

Six Little Preludes and Fugues

Prelude & Fugue One (1½ minutes)
Prelude & Fugue Three (1½ minutes)
Prelude & Fugue Six (2½ minutes)

These well-crafted little pieces are a fine example of contrapuntal writing, following the Baroque tradition of J.S. Bach.

Rate this piece: ☆☆☆☆☆

What I like about this piece:

How I would describe this piece (Prelude & Fugue 1):

How I would describe this piece (Prelude & Fugue 3):

How I would describe this piece (Prelude & Fugue 6):

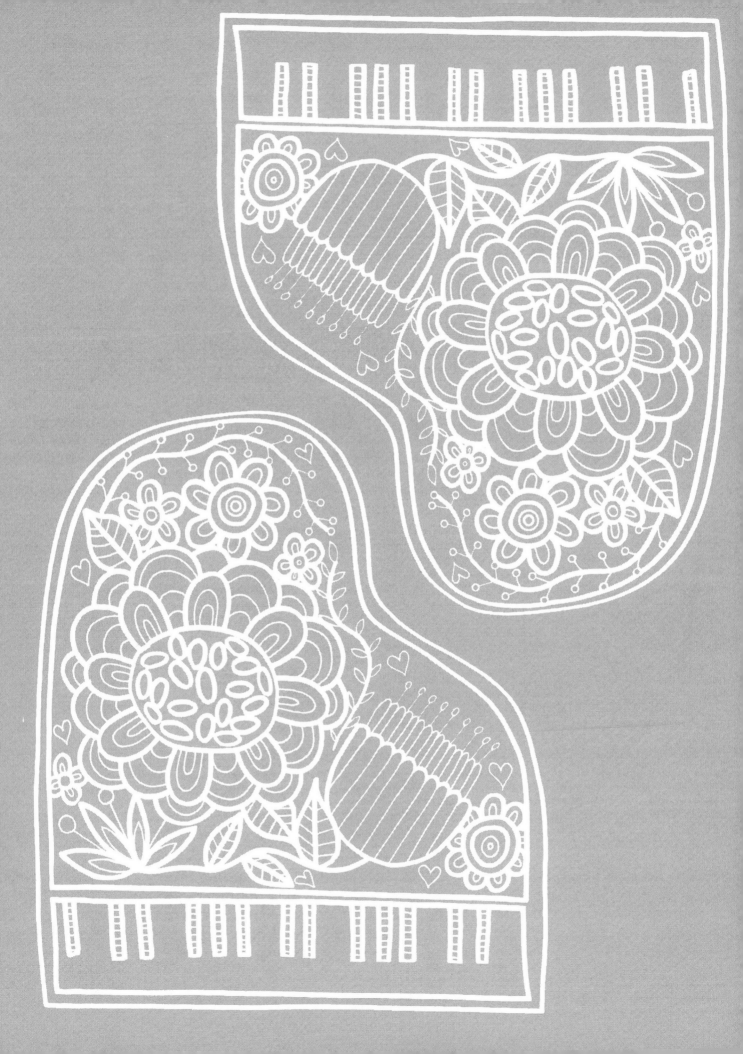

Jennifer Higdon

born 1962
United States

Jennifer Higdon is one of America's most acclaimed living composers and is a major figure in contemporary Classical music. Compared to other composers she got quite a late start in her musical journey; it started when she was fifteen when she taught herself the flute. At eighteen she began her formal music training, and then she started composing at twenty-one. She has a PhD and an MA in music composition and a BM in flute performance, as well as an Artist's Diploma in music composition.

Jennifer's works have been performed throughout the world, and they receive several hundred performances each year. Her works are featured on over sixty albums. Her orchestral work *blue cathedral* is one of the most-performed contemporary orchestral compositions by a living American. It has had over 600 performances all over the world since the year 2000.

Jennifer is a very prolific composer, with works in the genres of chamber, choral, vocal, orchestral, string, wind ensemble and band, and opera.

Piano Trio, I. Pale Yellow (8 minutes)

This piece for violin, cello and piano was written in 2003. The second movement is entitled *Fiery Red*. Jennifer says this about her composition: "I have always been fascinated with the connection between painting and music. In my composing, I often picture colors as if I were spreading them on a canvas, except I do so with melodies, harmonies and through the instruments themselves."

Rate this piece: ☆☆☆☆☆

What I like about this piece:	How I would describe this piece:

Listening Selections | Jennifer Higdon

Secret & Glass Gardens (9 minutes)

This is a work for solo piano. Here is what the composer says about this piece: "A journey of wonder and discovery, this secret garden reflects the paths of our hearts. It is a place of magical colors and brightly hued glass, where all is in view. The plants that grow there are like no other, in color and shape, and every turn of a corner brings new discoveries. The garden sweeps the viewer along amidst small, delicate details and full, grand shapes, carrying magic through all corners and at every step."

Rate this piece: ★ ☆ ☆ ☆ ☆

What I like about this piece:	How I would describe this piece:

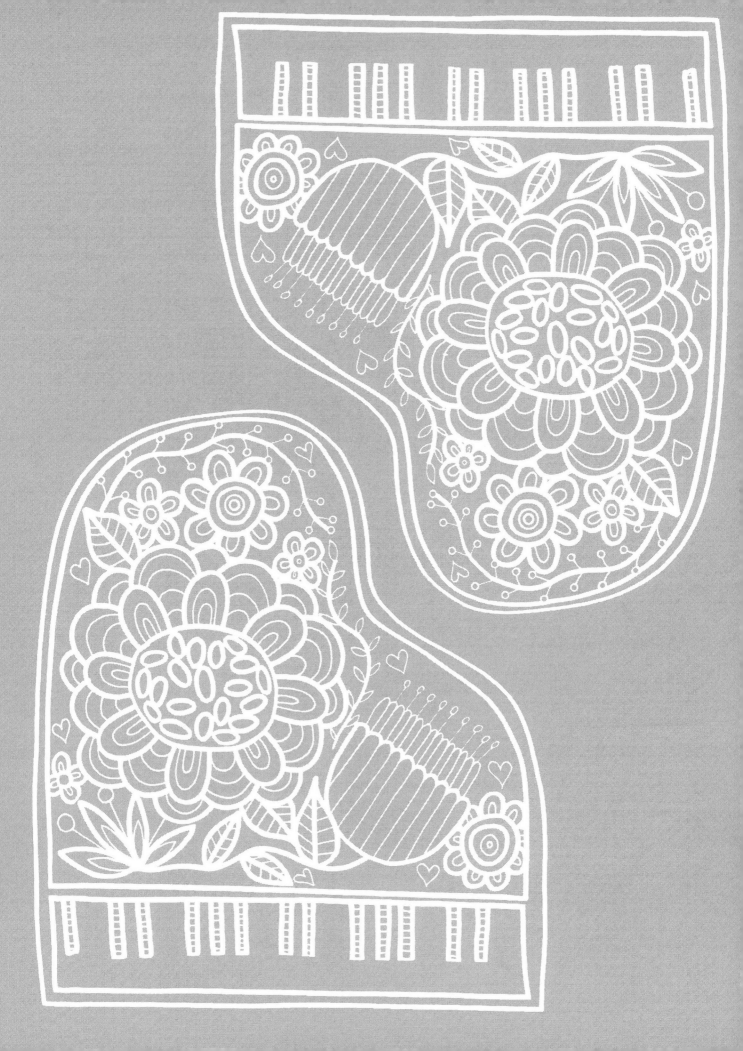

Natalie Klouda

born 1984
United Kingdom

Natalie Klouda is a British violinist and composer. She has performed in major venues throughout Europe as a chamber musician and was a founding member of an award-winning string quartet, the Finzi Quartet. She has composed works for solo violin as well as chamber music, including an Olympics-inspired quartet entitled *Five Rings*, which was commissioned to premiere in London during the 2012 Olympics.

Piano Trio No. 1 - *Fantasy Triptych*

I.   Explorations: Clara (5 minutes)

Klouda's Piano Trio No. 1 was written for an album entitled *Triptych*, featuring music of three women composers in three different centuries, played by the three players of the Monte Piano Trio. Each movement of this *Fantasy Triptych* is dedicated to the historical trio of musicians Robert and Clara Schumann and Johannes Brahms. This movement, *Explorations: Clara*, explores the life of Clara Schumann. At times achingly sad and sometimes other-worldly, the music is a fitting study of the probable troubled emotions of the repressed composer and wife of Robert Schumann.

Rate this piece: ★ ☆ ☆ ☆ ☆

What I like about this piece:

How I would describe this piece:

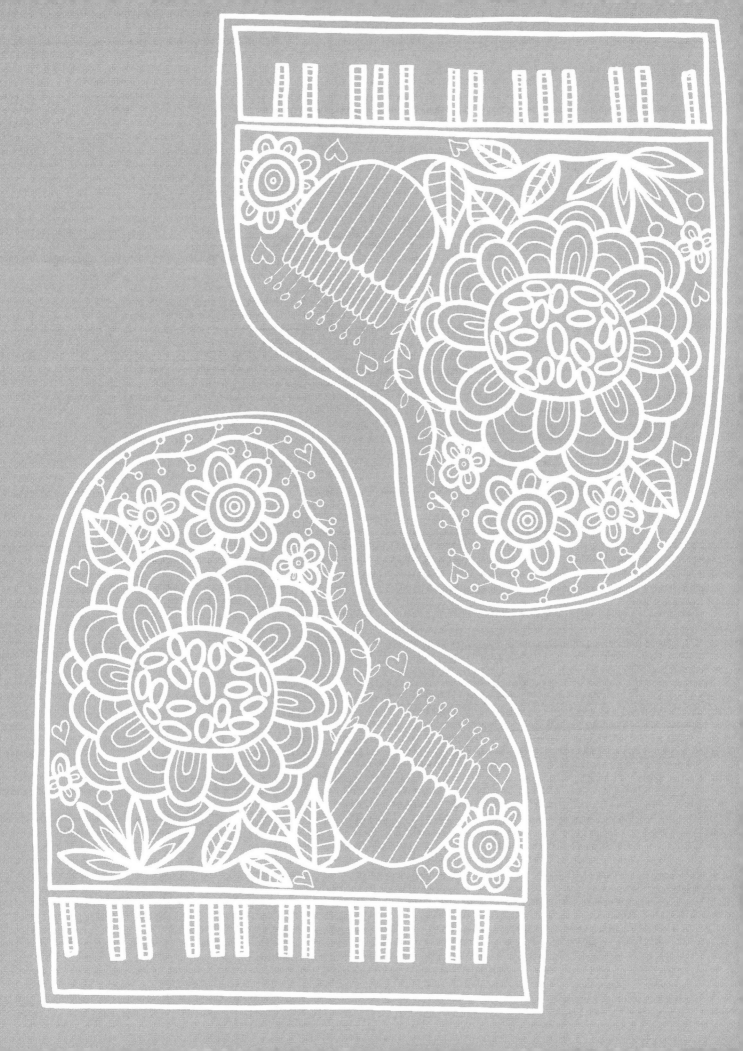

Kristina Arakelyan

born 1994
Hungary

Kristina Arakelyan is a young Armenian pianist and award-winning composer who was born in Budapest, Hungary. She studied composition at the Royal Academy of Music and the University of Oxford. Her compositions have been heard in concert halls in the United Kingdom, Mexico, Spain, Belgium, Croatia and Armenia.

Her works include choral works, chamber music, and works for symphony orchestra and solo piano.

To the Stars (4 1/2 minutes)

This piece for solo piano has an ethereal and impressionistic quality to it. It has some modern-sounding dissonant harmonies, but not so many that it is inaccessible to the average listener.

Rate this piece: ★ ☆ ☆ ☆ ☆

What I like about this piece:	How I would describe this piece:

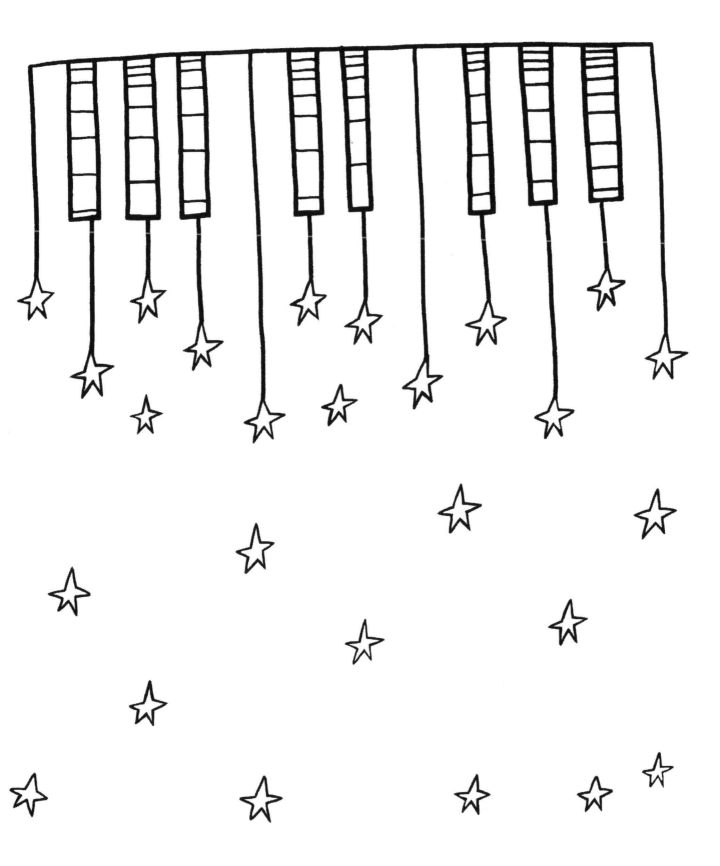

Glossary

basso continuo	An independent bass line continuing throughout a piece of music that helps form the foundation of the music. This would often be performed on a harpsichord, and filled out with chords indicated by the score.
cantata	A composition for voices and instrumental accompaniment, usually including solos, duets, recitatives and choruses.
chant	To sing a single pitch or a limited range of pitches repetitively.
chromatic scale	A scale that includes all twelve pitches contained in an octave, or in other words all white and black keys on the piano.
chromaticism	The use of some pitches of the chromatic scale along with those of the diatonic scale.
concerto	A multi-movement instrumental work for a soloist accompanied by an orchestra.
consonance	Two or more notes that sound stable together, not needing to be resolved. These intervals sound pleasant and agreeable.
contrapuntal	Having the characteristics of *counterpoint* – the combination of two or more melodic lines sounding together.
convent	An establishment of nuns.
curtain call	An appearance by a performer at the end of a performance in response to the audience's applause.
diatonic scale	A scale that includes seven notes per octave, arranged in patterns of half and whole steps. Includes major and natural minor scales and church modes.

dissonance	Two or more notes that sound unstable together, needing to be resolved. These intervals sound tense.
encore	An extra piece played at the end of a concert by demand of the audience.
flautist	One who plays the flute.
Goethe	Johann Wolfgang von Goethe was a German writer who wrote novels, poetry, drama, memoirs and more.
harpsichord	A stringed keyboard instrument, similar in shape to the grand piano, in use from the 16th through 18th centuries. Notes were sounded by a mechanism that would pluck the strings (as opposed to a hammer striking the strings in a piano).
improvisation	Composing or making up music as it is being played.
John Field	An Irish composer and pianist who was known for his piano nocturnes.
King Louis XIV	Also known as Louis the Great or the Sun King, King Louis XIV was king of France for over 70 years. He ruled from his great palace of Versailles and was a symbol of absolute monarchy.
lieder	German poems set to music. These lyric songs consist of solo voice accompanied by piano and were popular during the Classical and Romantic period.
liturgical	Having to do with the church services of the Christian church.
manuscript	A hand-written composition.
mazurka	A Polish folk dance in triple time that originated in the province of Mazovia near Warsaw. Mazurkas in art music have strong contrasts in tempo, an expressive character and a slight rhythmic lilt.
melisma	A single syllable of text sung while moving between several different notes.

mode	A type of musical scale (or a series of musical pitches in an order) that has certain melodic characteristics. The major mode and minor mode are two examples of modes, but there are many others, each with their own distinct sound.
monophonic	Music made up of a single melody without accompaniment.
nocturne	A type of instrumental work popular in the 19th and 20th centuries, usually for solo piano, that contains a lyrical melody accompanied by broken chords. The mood of these works is often evocative of the night.
ornaments	Musical flourishes or embellishments; added notes that are not needed in the melody but act as decorations that add variety to the music. Examples of ornaments include trills, mordents, and grace notes.
pentatonic scale	A scale consisting of five notes per octave.
plainsong	Monophonic Christian liturgical chant written in free rhythm.
polonaise	A festive, processional Polish folk dance performed by couples at a moderate tempo. A polonaise is usually in triple meter and includes short repeated sections.
prodigy	A highly talented child.
salon	A popular gathering of people where music was performed in an intimate setting. Salons flourished in France during the 17th and 18th centuries and were often run by women.
scherzo	Italian for "joke," a scherzo is a type of piece that is in fast ¾ time. Scherzi are often light and playful but can also be menacing and grim.
sonata	A musical work for one or more instruments, in the Baroque period usually with one to four melody instruments and basso continuo. A sonata usually had several movements.
tithe	A tenth part of something paid voluntarily, usually to a religious organization.

viola da gamba — A 16th and 17th century bowed string instrument played on or between the legs. The viola de gamba looks similar to a modern-day cello, but it has more strings, is tuned differently, has a quieter sound and the bow is held underhand.

whole-tone scale — A scale consisting only of whole steps. A whole-tone scale consists of six notes per octave. There are only two possible whole-tone scales: C D E F# G# A# and C# D# F G A B.

Bibliography

Alexina Louie. "Alexina Louie: Bio." alexinalouie.ca. http://www.alexinalouie.ca/bio (Accessed February 14, 2018).

Alexina Louie. "Alexina Louie: Catalouge." alexinalouie.ca. http://www.alexinalouie.ca/catalogue (Accessed February 14, 2018).

Beer, Anna. *Sounds and Sweet Airs: The Forgotten Women of Classical Music*, Reprint Edition. London: Oneworld Publications, 2017.

Cecilia McDowall. "Cecilia McDowall: Biography." ceciliamcdowall.co.uk. http://www.ceciliamcdowall.co.uk/biography (Accessed February 17, 2018).

Cecilia McDowall. "Cecilia McDowall: Instrumental Works." ceciliamcdowall.co.uk. http://www.ceciliamcdowall.co.uk/works/instrumental (Accessed February 17, 2018).

Cowan, Rob. "Triptych." gramophone.co.uk. https://www.gramophone.co.uk/review/triptych (Accessed June 8, 2018).

Curtis, Liane. "Rebecca Clarke: Viola Music." Naxos.com. https://www.naxos.com/mainsite/blurbs_reviews.asp?item_code=8.557934&catNum=557934&filetype=About%20this%20Recording&language=English (Accessed September 28, 2018).

Erlanger, Philippe. "Louis XIV." Brittanica. https://www.britannica.com/biography/Louis-XIV-king-of-France (Accessed September 19, 2018).

Hayman, Sheila. "A Fanny Mendelssohn masterpiece finally gets its due." theguardian.com. https://www.theguardian.com/music/2017/mar/08/fanny-mendelssohn-easter-sonata-premiere-sheila-hayman (Accessed February 15, 2018).

Hinson, Maurice, and Wesley Roberts. *Guide to the Pianist's Repertoire*, Fourth Edition, Kindle Edition. Bloomington: Indiana University Press, 2014.

Jennifer Higdon. "Jennifer Higdon: Biography." jenniferhigdon.com. http://jenniferhigdon.com/biography.html (Accessed February 17, 2018).

Jennifer Higdon. "Jennifer Higdon: Chamber Works." jenniferhigdon.com. http://jenniferhigdon.com/chamberworks.html (Accessed February 17, 2018).

Jezic, Diane Peacock. *Women Composers: The Lost Tradition Found*, Second Edition. New York: The Feminist Press at CUNY, 1994.

Judith Lang Zaimont. "Artist Biography." judithzaimont.com. https://www.judithzaimont.com/full-bio-final.html (Accessed June 13, 2018).

Judith Lang Zaimont. "Keyboard Music." judithzaimont.com. https://www.judithzaimont.com/keyboard.html (Accessed June 13, 2018).

June Armstrong. "June Armstrong: About the composer." junearmstrong.com. https://www.junearmstrong.com/about-the-composer/ (Accessed February 17, 2018).

Kristina Arakelyan. "Kristina Arakelyan: Biography." kristinaarakelyan.com. https://www.kristinaarakelyan.com/biography (Accessed June 11, 2018).

Merriam Webster. https://www.merriam-webster.com (Accessed September 19, 2018).

Music of Armenia. "Kristina Arakelyan." musicofarmenia.com. http://www.musicofarmenia.com/kristinaarakelyan (Accessed June 11, 2018).

Natalie Klouda. "Natalie Klouda: Biography." natalieklouda.com. https://www.natalieklouda.com/biography (Accessed June 11, 2018).

Philips, Nicholas. "Music for the intermediate pianist by eight women composers." claviercompanion.com. https://www.claviercompanion.com/current-issue/music-for-the-intermediate-pianist-by-eight-women-composers (Accessed February 17, 2018).

Randel, Don Michael, ed. *The Harvard Concise Dictionary of Music and Musicians*. Cambridge, Massachusetts: The Belknap Press of Harvard University Press, 1999.

Rebecca Clarke Society. "Rebecca Clarke." Rebeccaclarke.org. https://www.rebeccaclarke.org (Accessed September 28, 2018).

Rupp, Teresa. "Women of exceptional accomplishment: Eight women composers." claviercompanion.com. https://www.claviercompanion.com/current-issue/women-of-exceptional-accomplishment-eight-women-composers (Accessed February 17, 2018).

Sadie, Julie Anne and Rhian Samuel, ed. *The Norton/Grove Dictionary of Women Composers*. New York, New York: W. W. Norton & Company, 1995.

Did you enjoy this book?
Please help me get the word out by
leaving me an Amazon review!

Check out the other Shades of Sound
Listening & Coloring Books in the series!

Shades of Sound: Halloween
Shades of Sound: Christmas
Shades of Sound: Valentines Day

More titles coming soon!

Discover More Great Piano Teaching Resources at
theplayfulpiano.com

Save 10% at theplayfulpiano.com with coupon code
WOMENCOMPOSE

About the Author

Jenny Boster has been playing the piano and drawing ever since she was a little girl. She loves combining her interests to create fun and original resources for piano teachers. She has loved teaching piano lessons for twenty years! Jenny has a Bachelor of Music degree in Piano Performance from Brigham Young University and is a Nationally-Certified Teacher of Music. Jenny is passionate about encouraging students to listen to and gain a love for classical music. Her greatest joys are her husband, Jonathan, and being a mother to her five children. In fact, much of this book was written and planned out while snuggling with her newborn daughter, Annie.

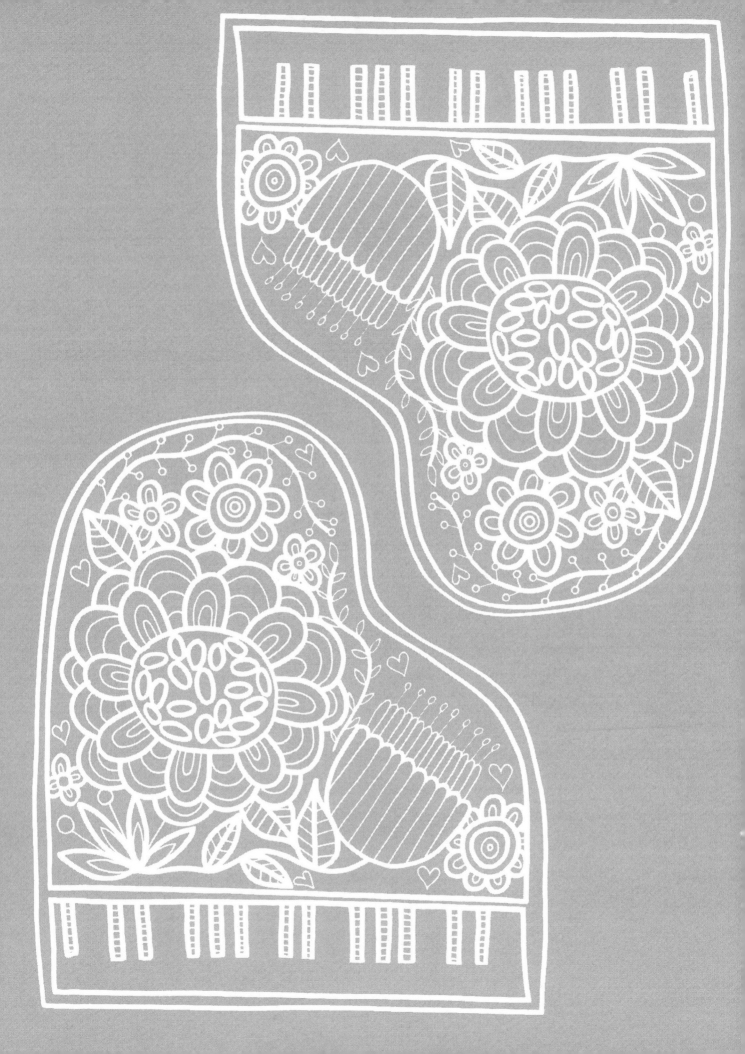

Made in the USA
Columbia, SC
19 December 2019